Grayscale
ADULT COLORING BOOKS
Nature

By Beth Ingrias

Want to color more for FREE?

Get a FREE 25 page adult coloring book

visit

www.BethIngrias.com

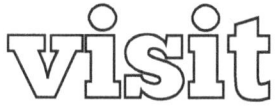

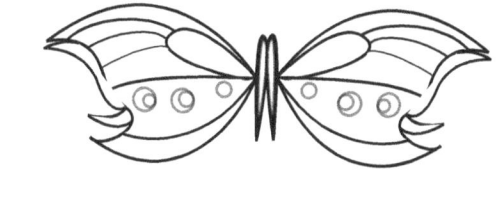

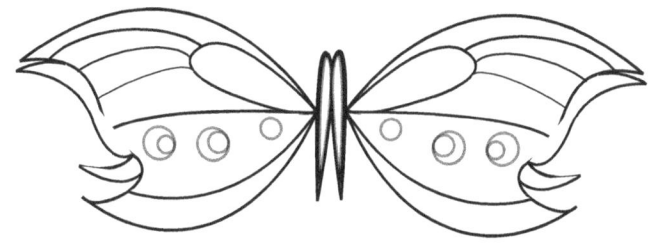

ISBN-13: 978-1533034274
ISBN-10: 1533034273

A Sample of What's Inside

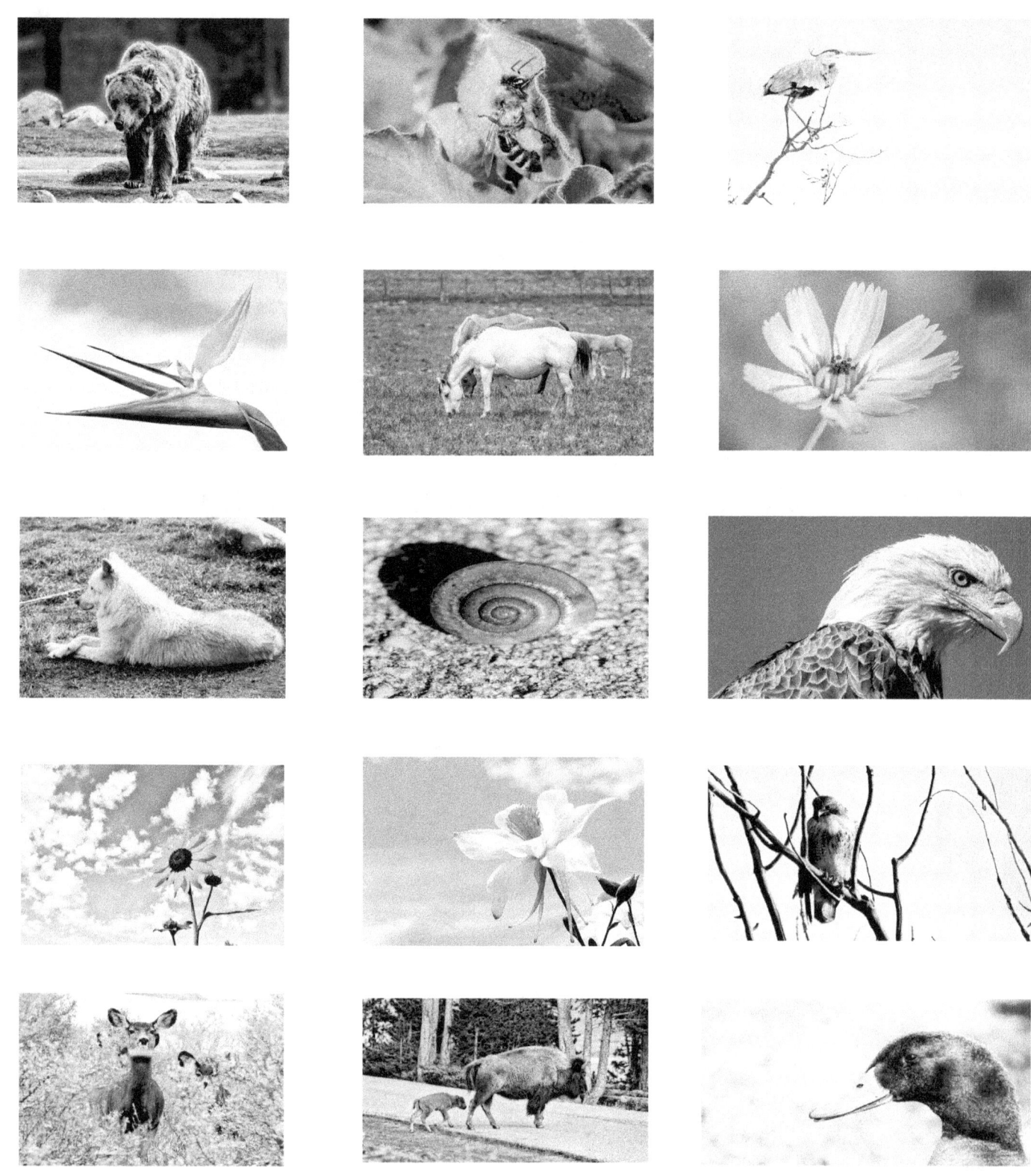

Coloring grayscale images is an easy way to create a work of art without hitting that creative roadblock that often appears when it is time to start adding depth with shading. All of the shading is already in place on the image. All you need to do is add your favorite colors.

You could think of this type of coloring as shading with training wheels. Not only is it very easy to get excellent results, but you can also learn quite a bit about how light, shadows and shading help to add depth to an image. Don't fight the gray areas. Use them to your advantage to give your work of art depth.

I highly recommend coloring these pages with markers. Use darker colors in the darker areas and light colors in the lighter areas. If you find that your finished piece is still too dark, you can go back over the lighter areas with colored pencils.

To make the entire process easier for you, each image is printed several times on one page before the full page version. Use these smaller images as a test color playground to determine which colors will work best before moving on to the full page images in the book.

You won't find these images anywhere else. When I am not creating adult coloring books, I am traveling and taking thousands of photos. Each image in this book comes from my personal collection of photos.

Have fun and enjoy!

Beth

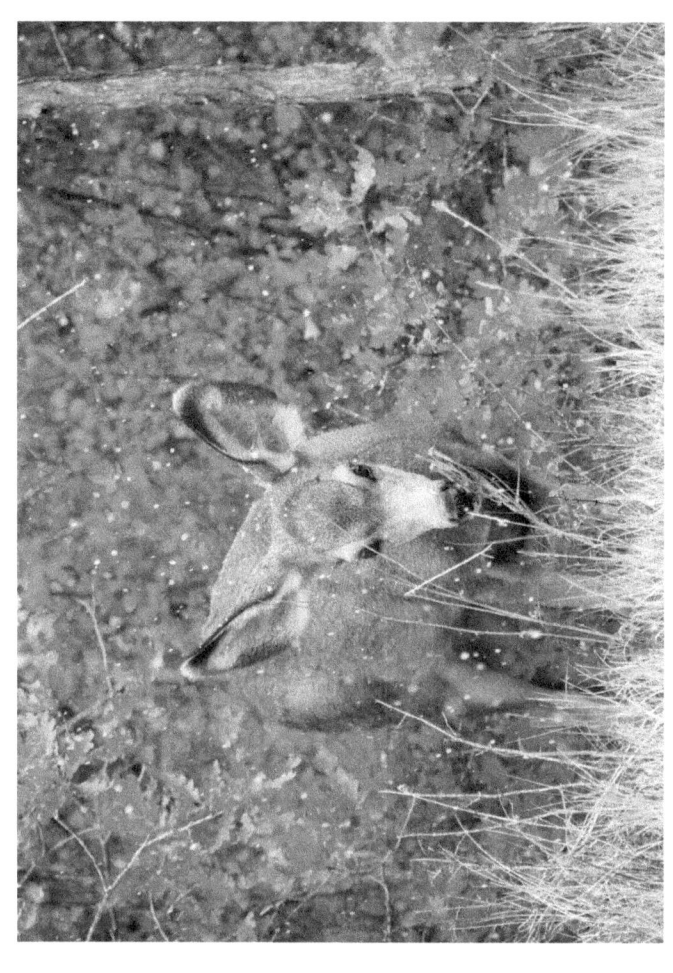 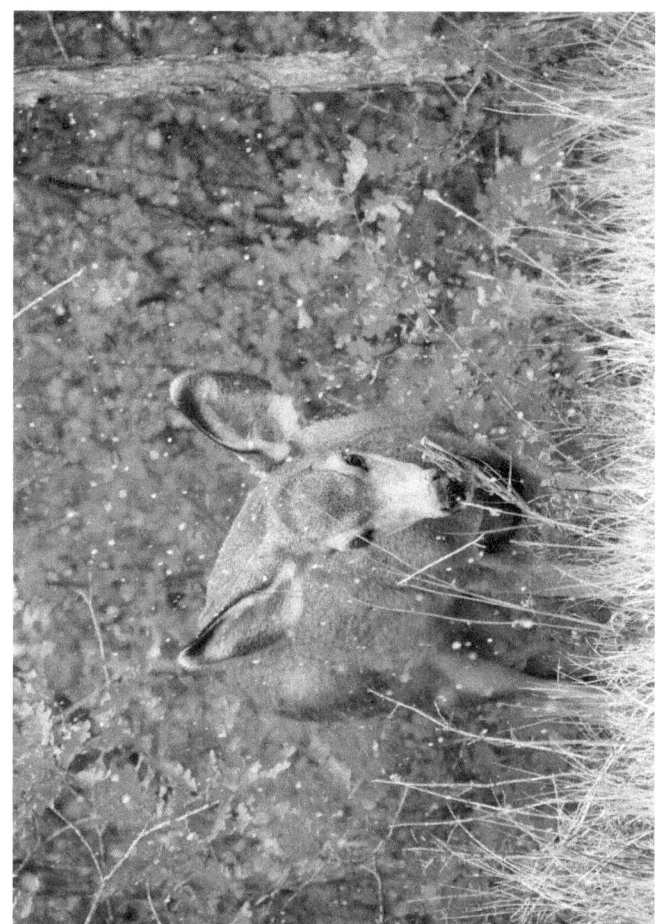

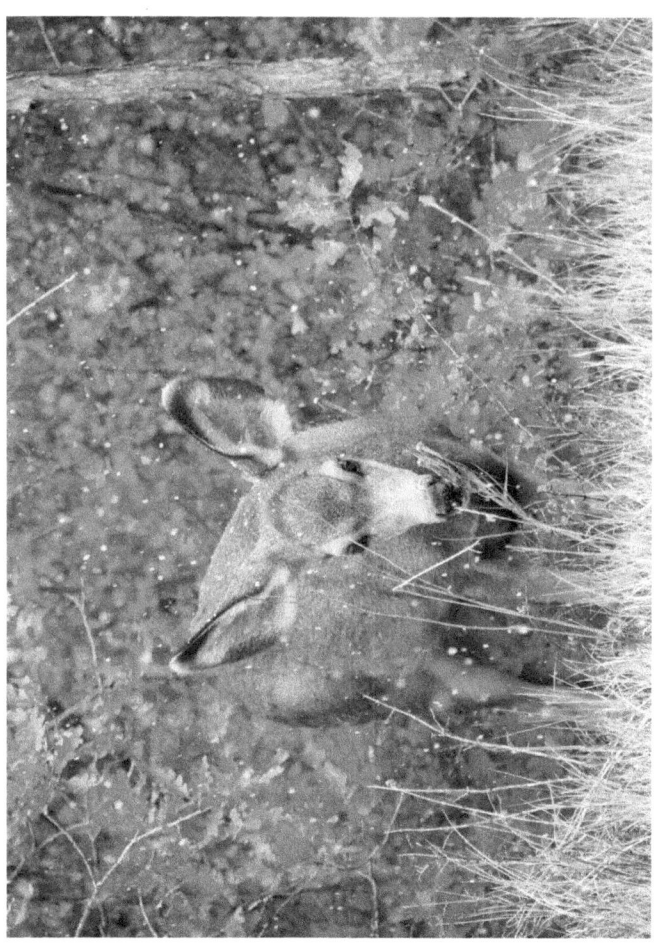 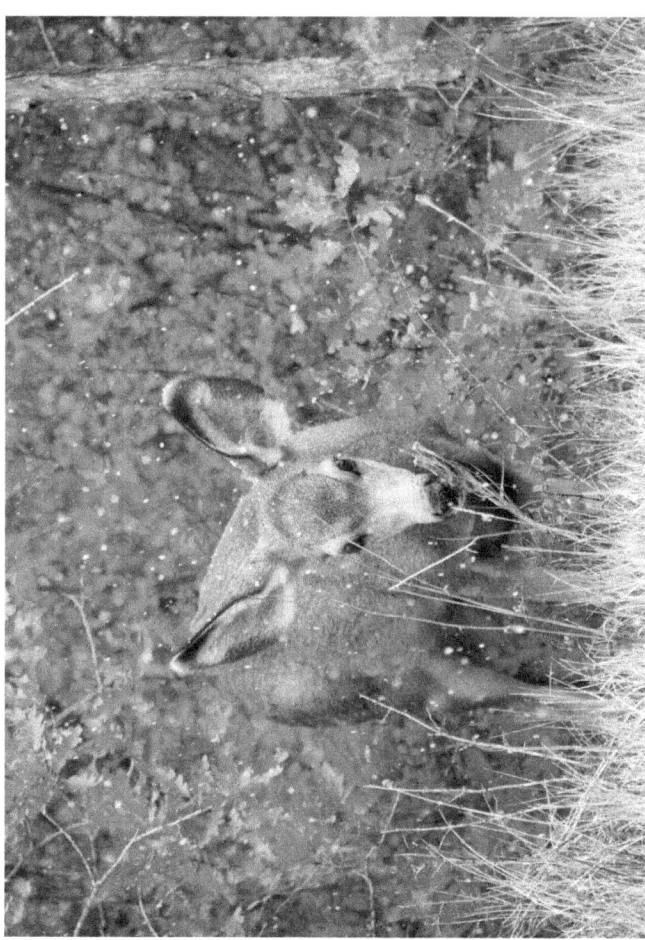

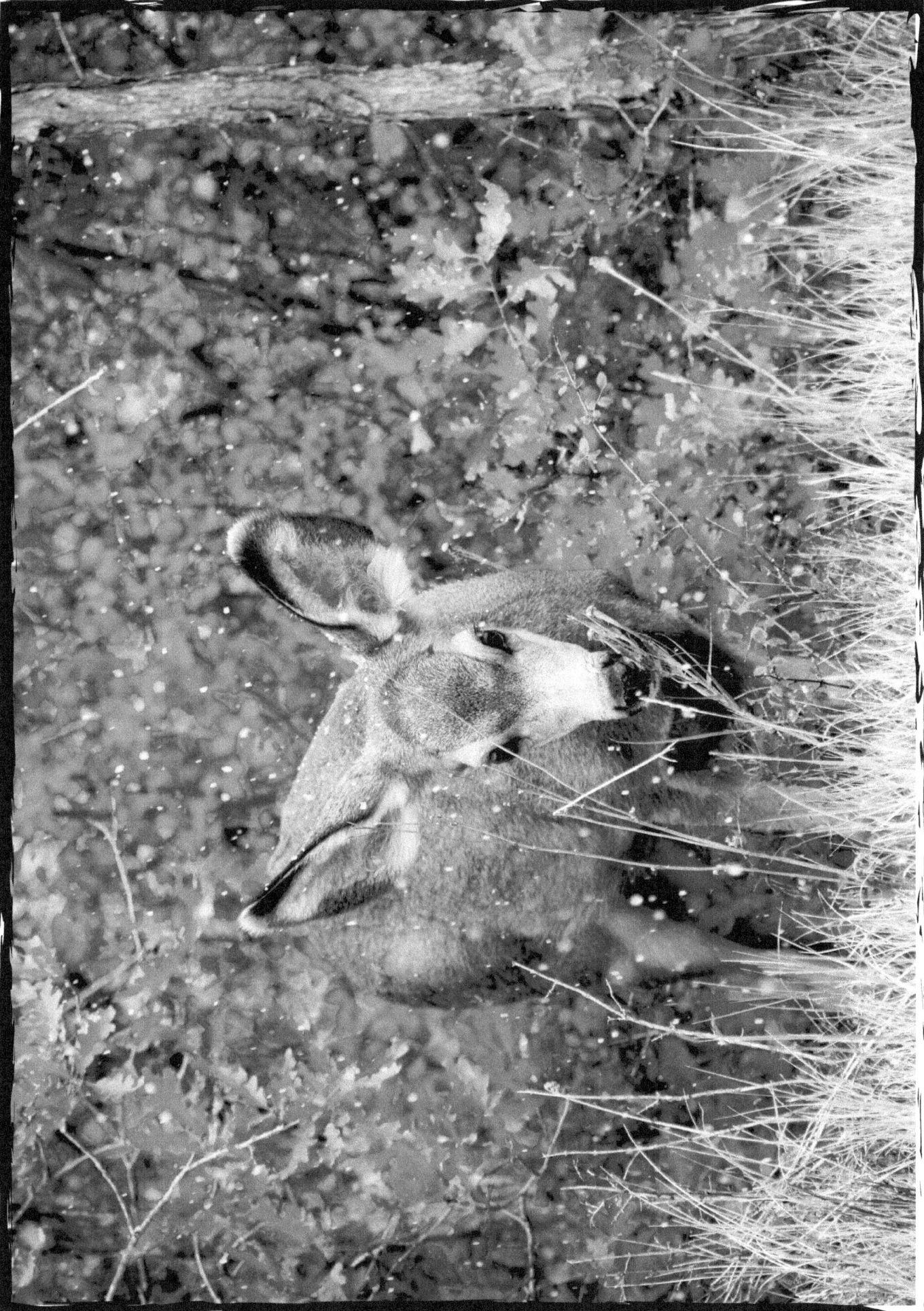

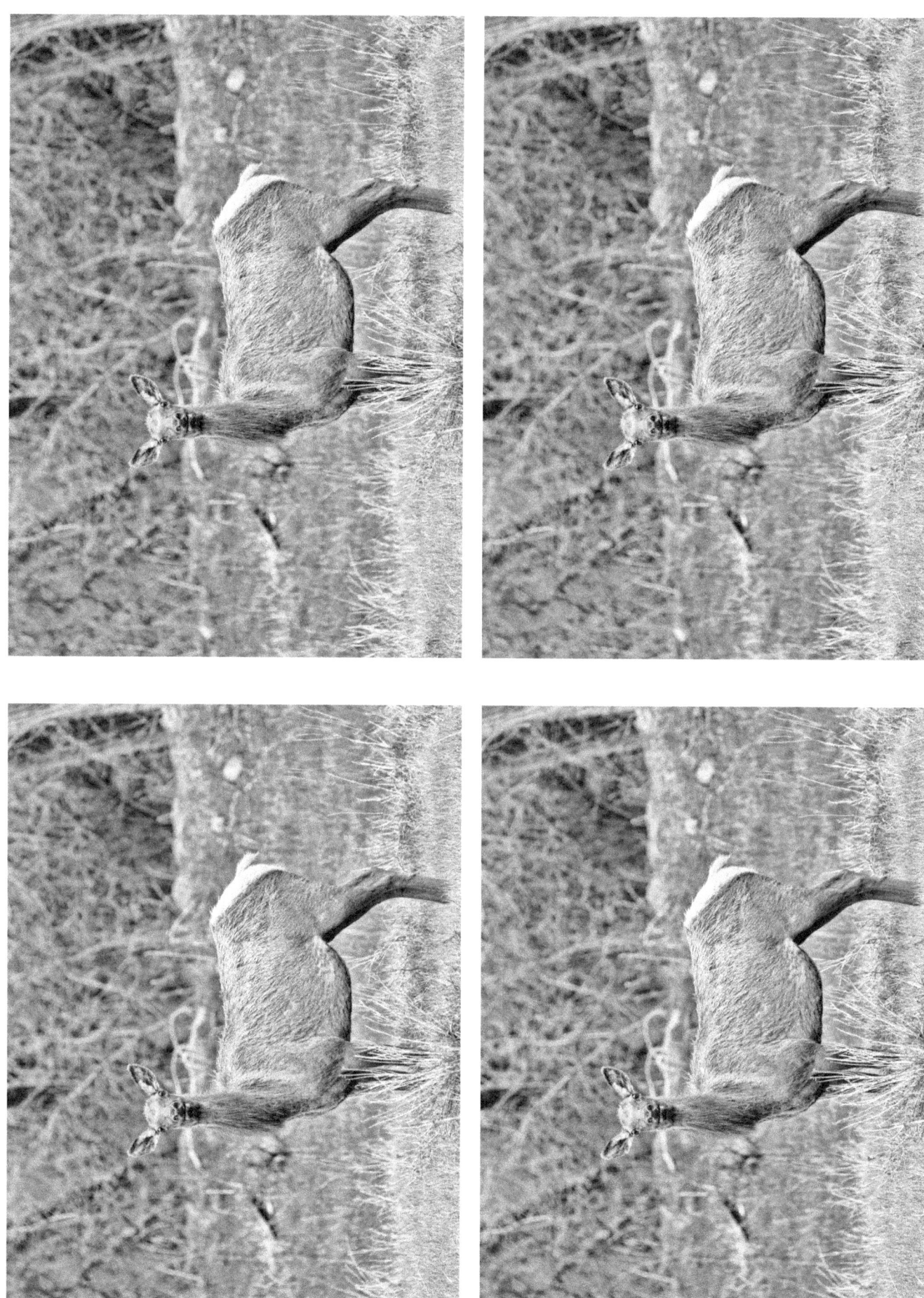

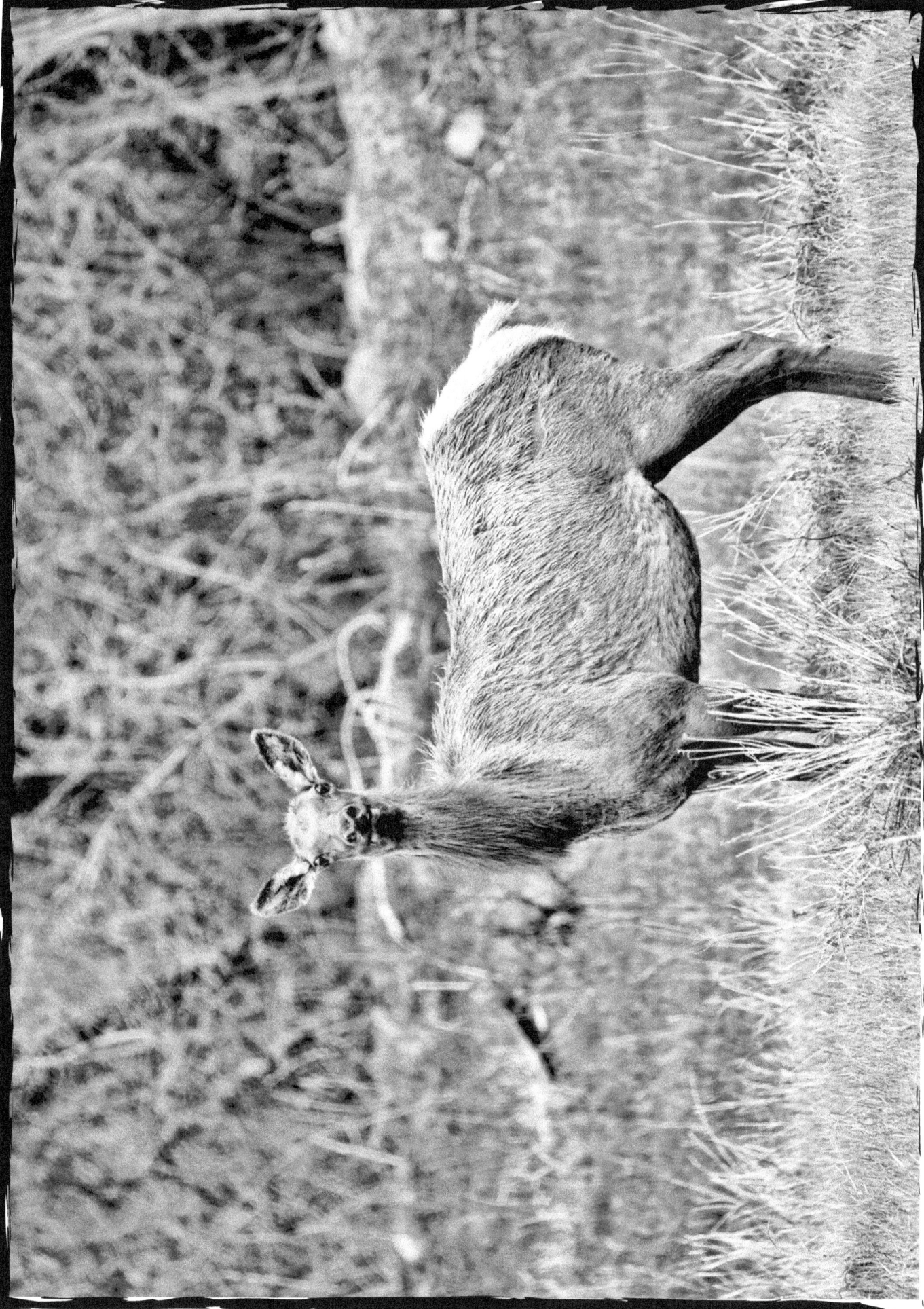

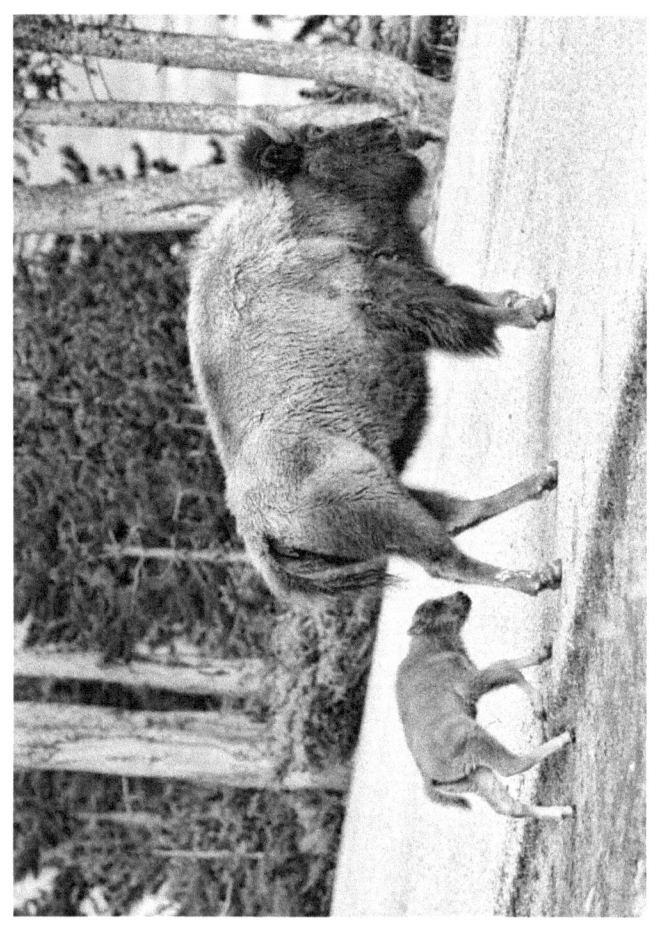
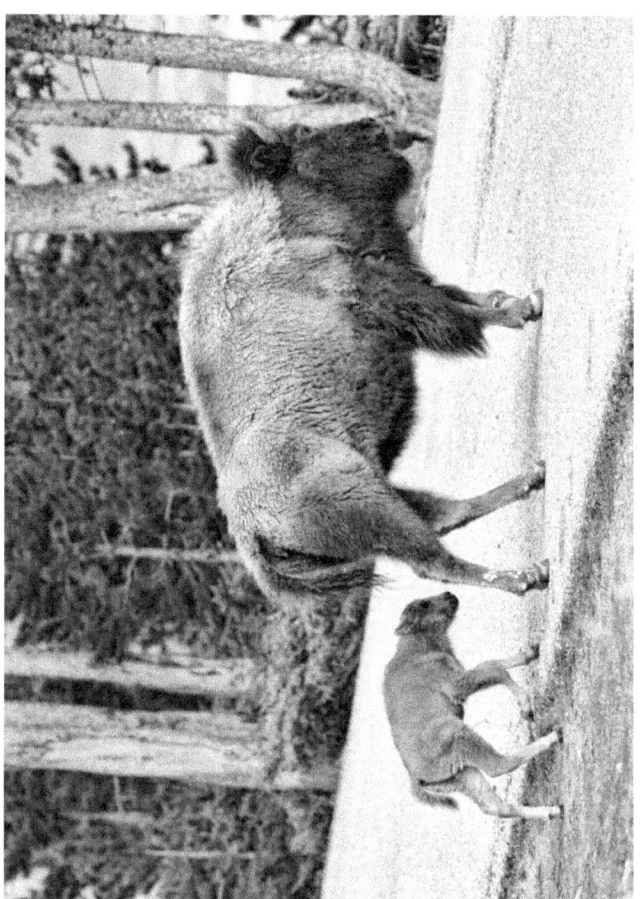
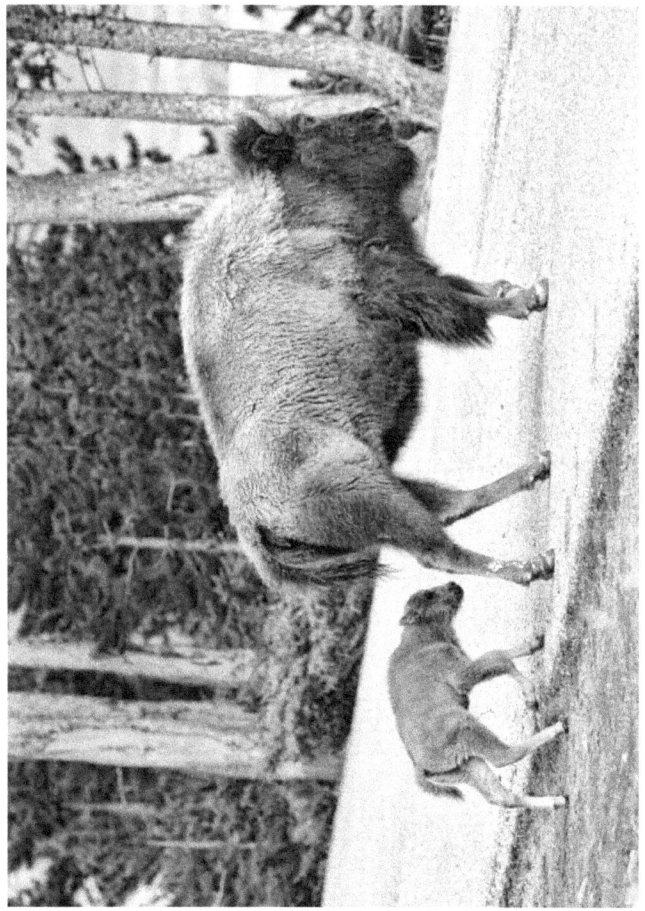
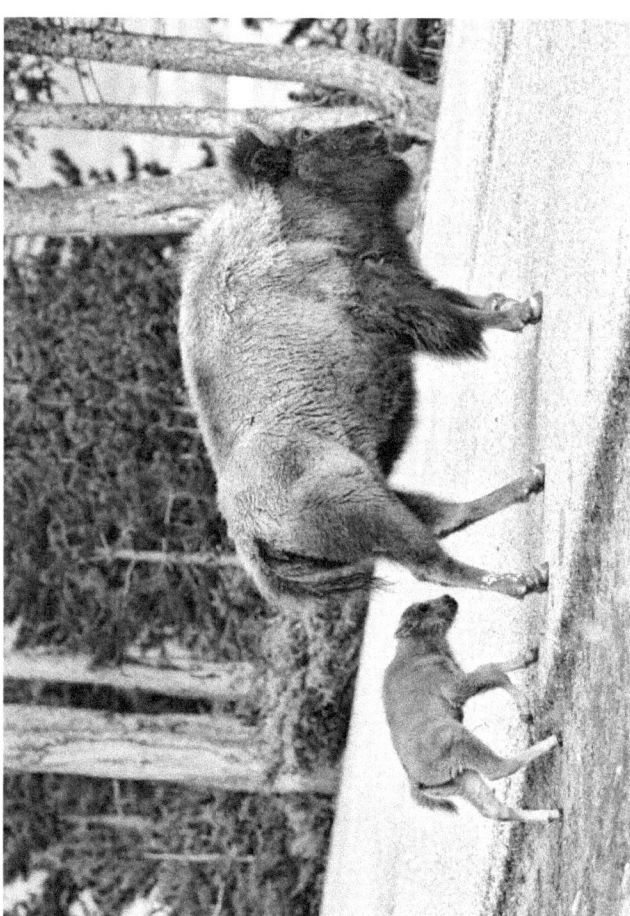

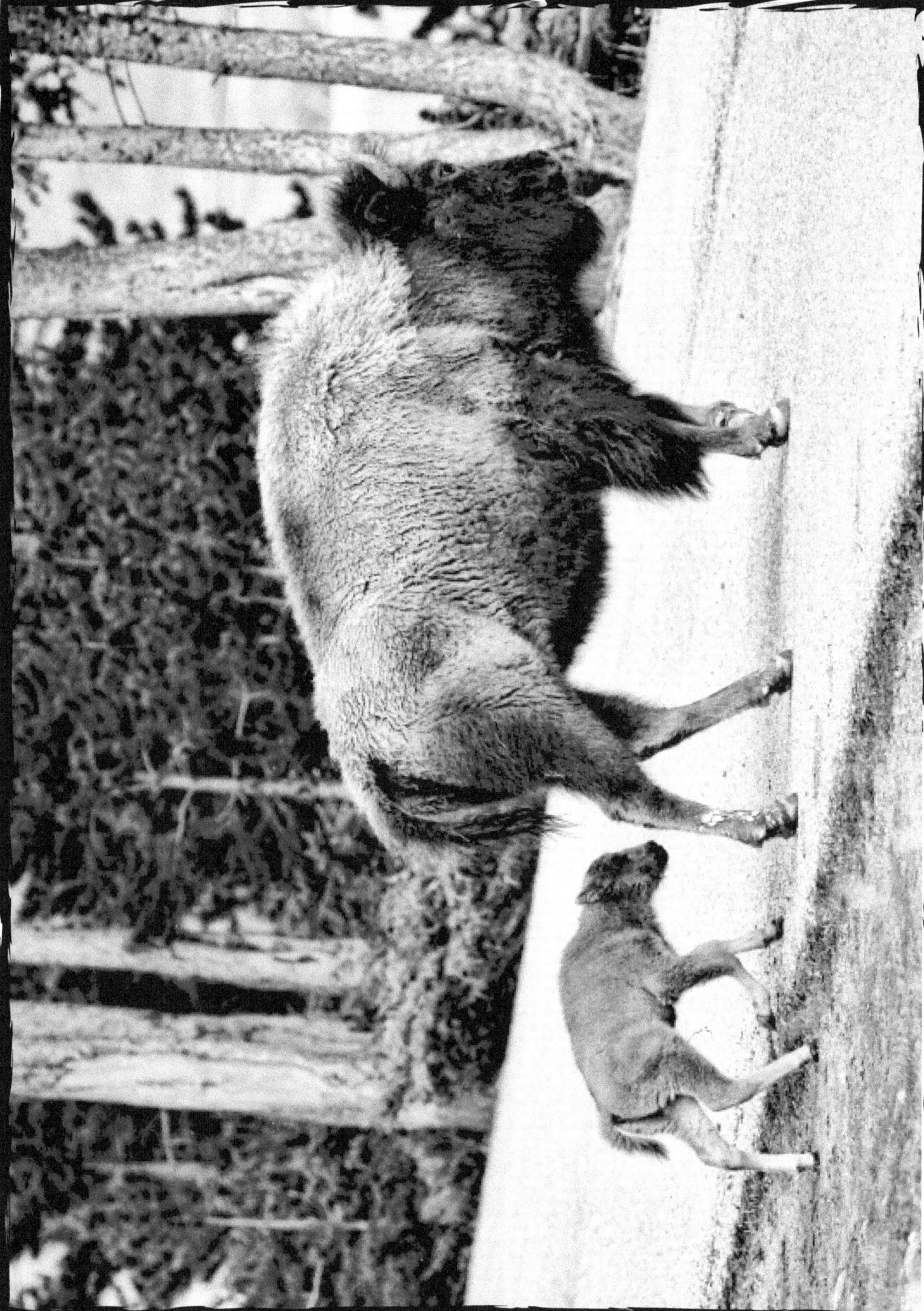

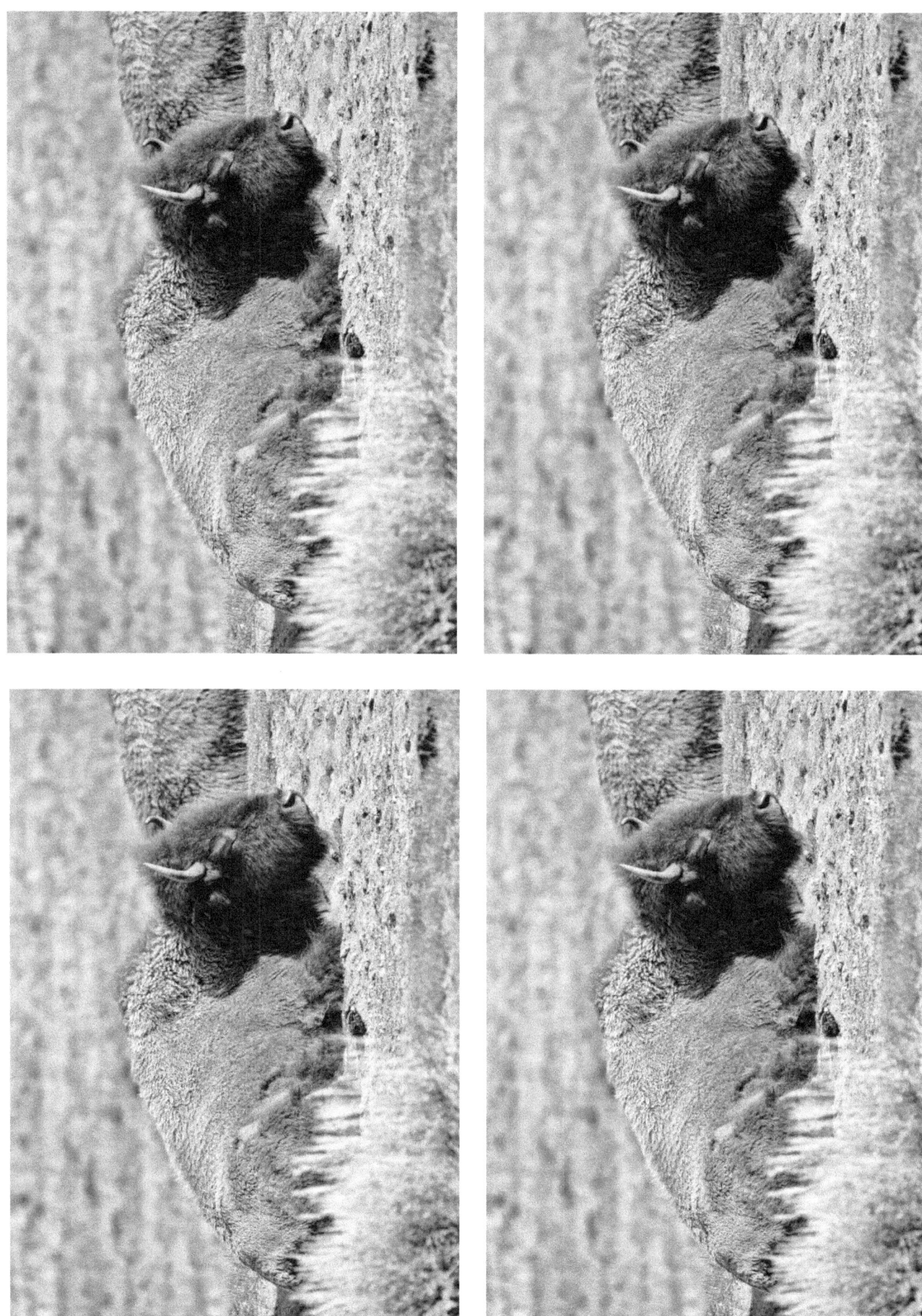

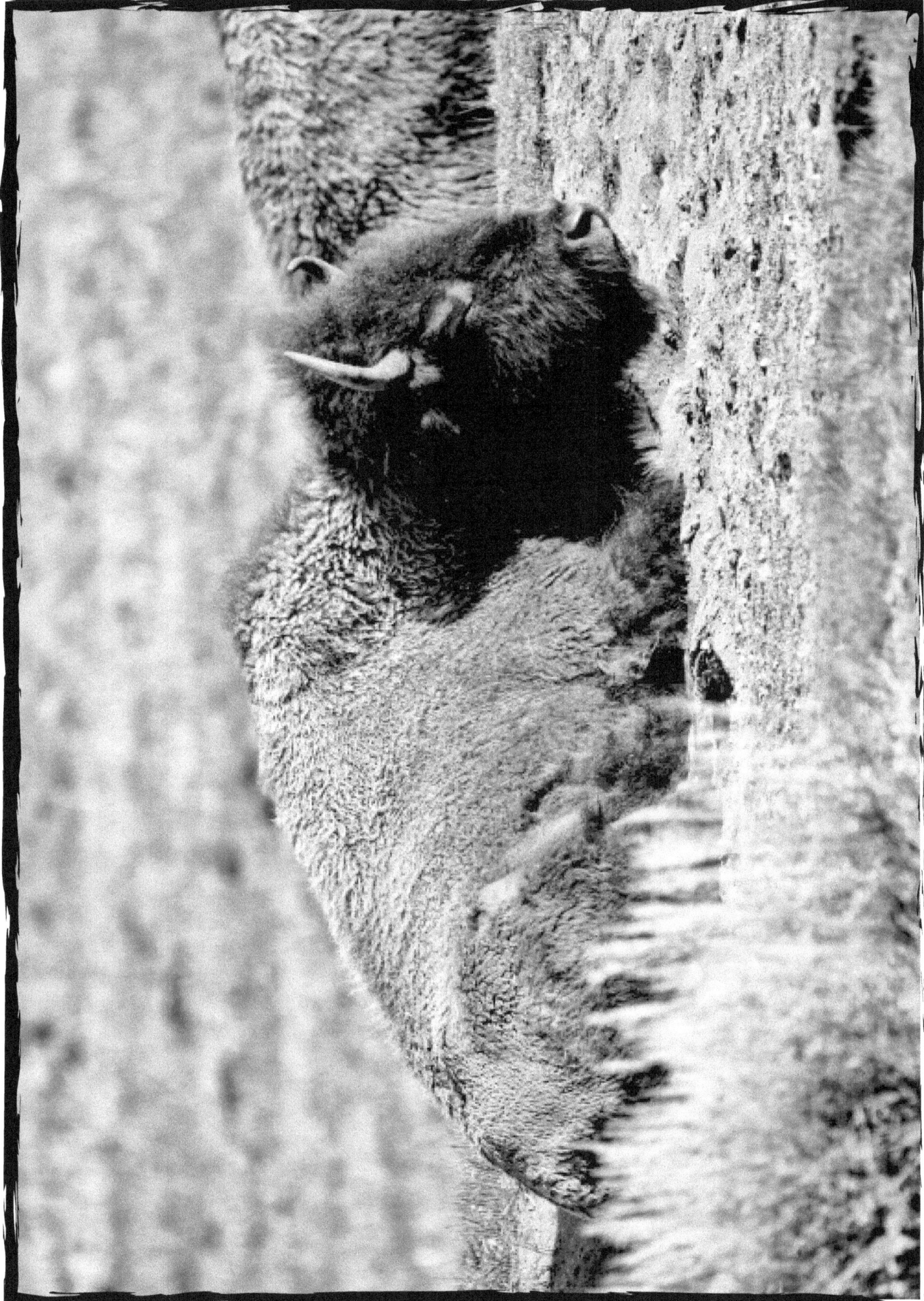

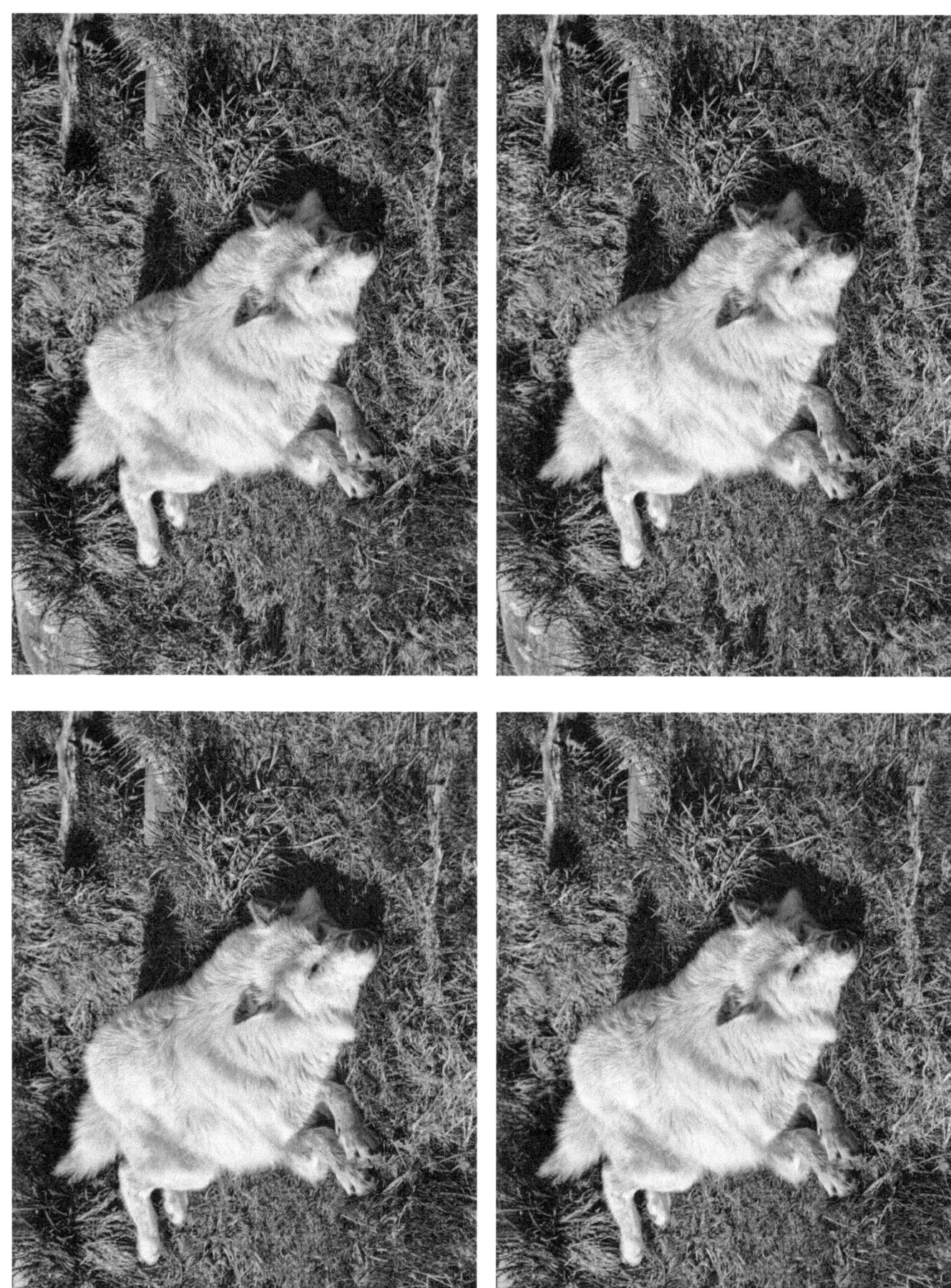

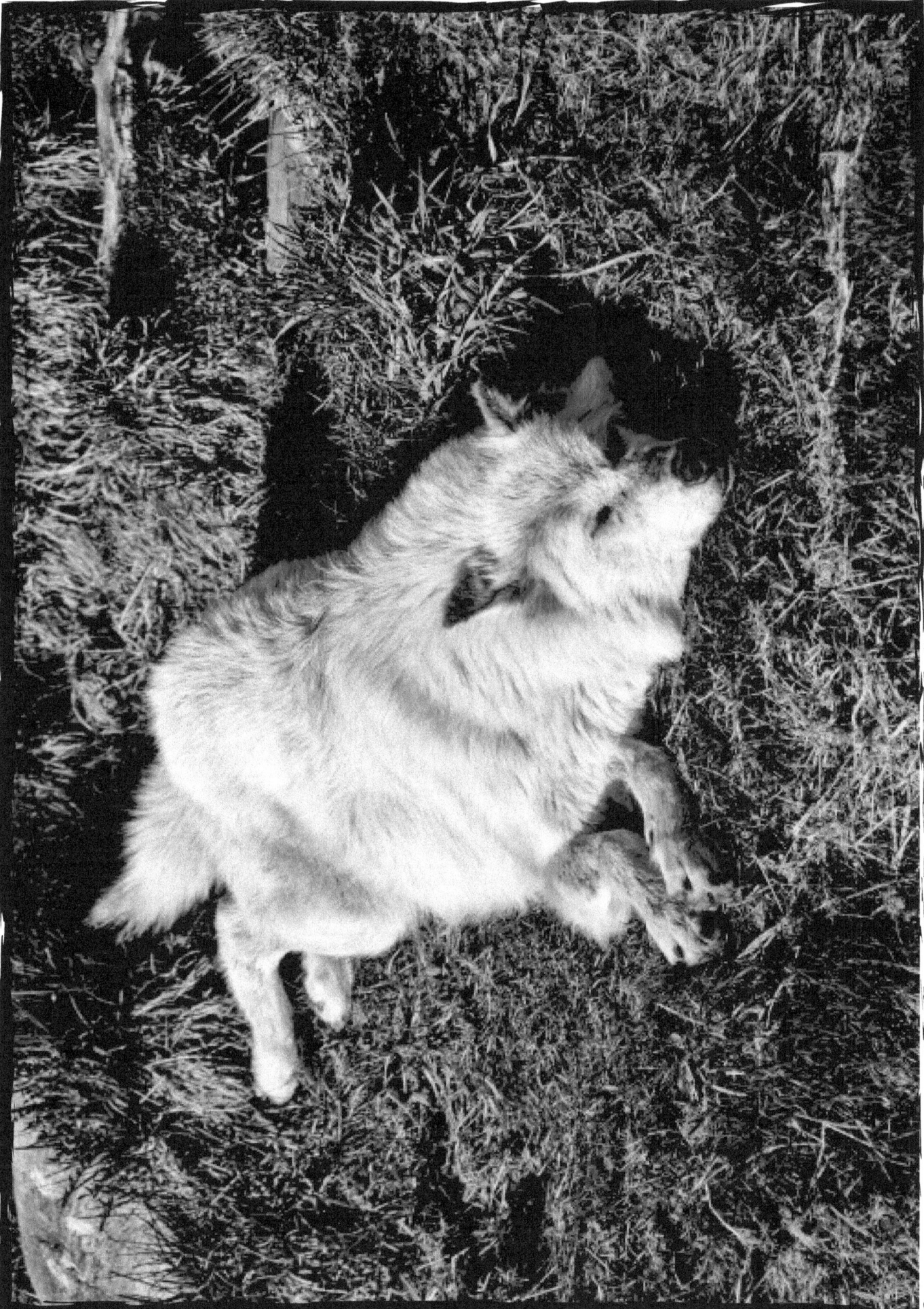

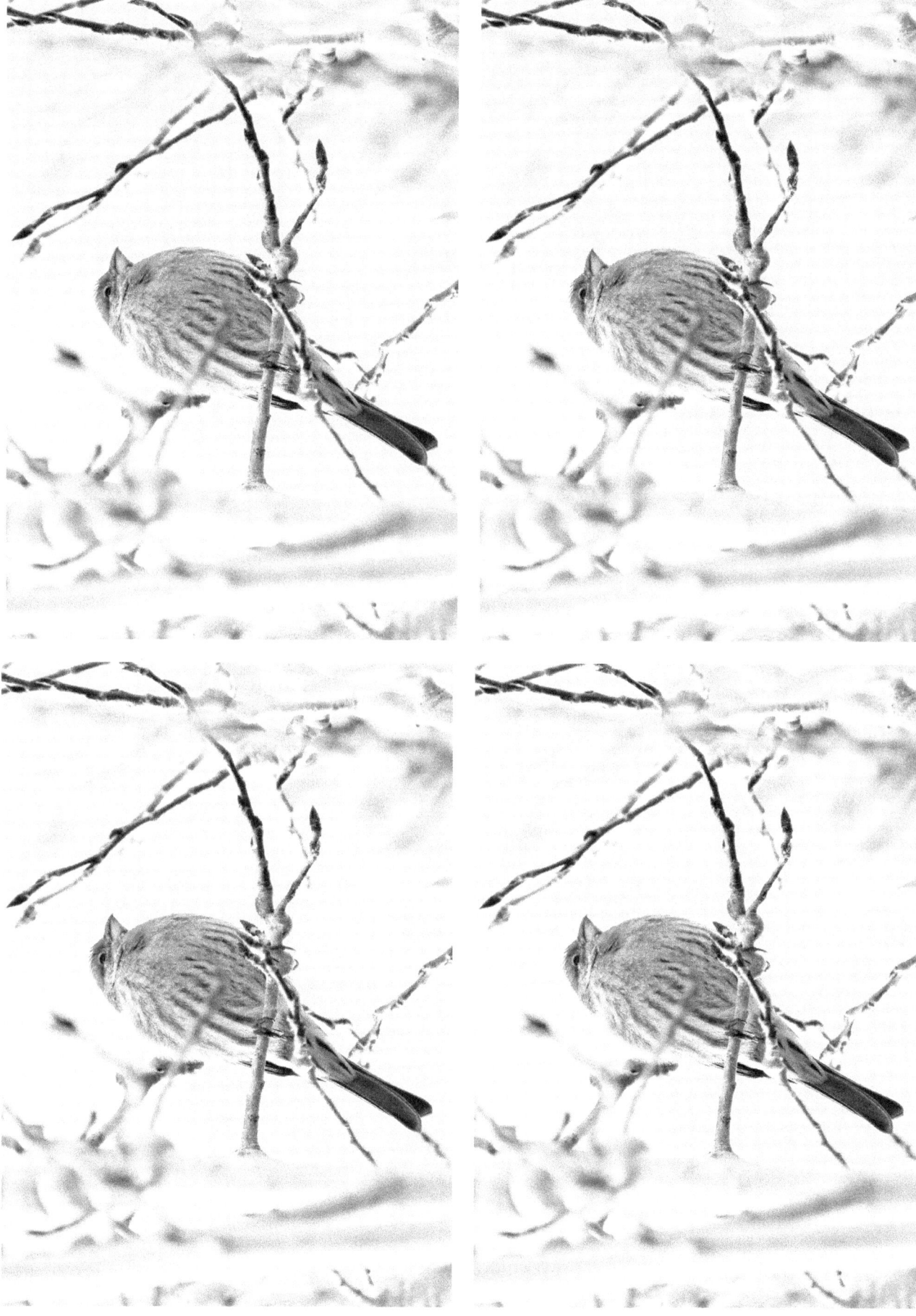

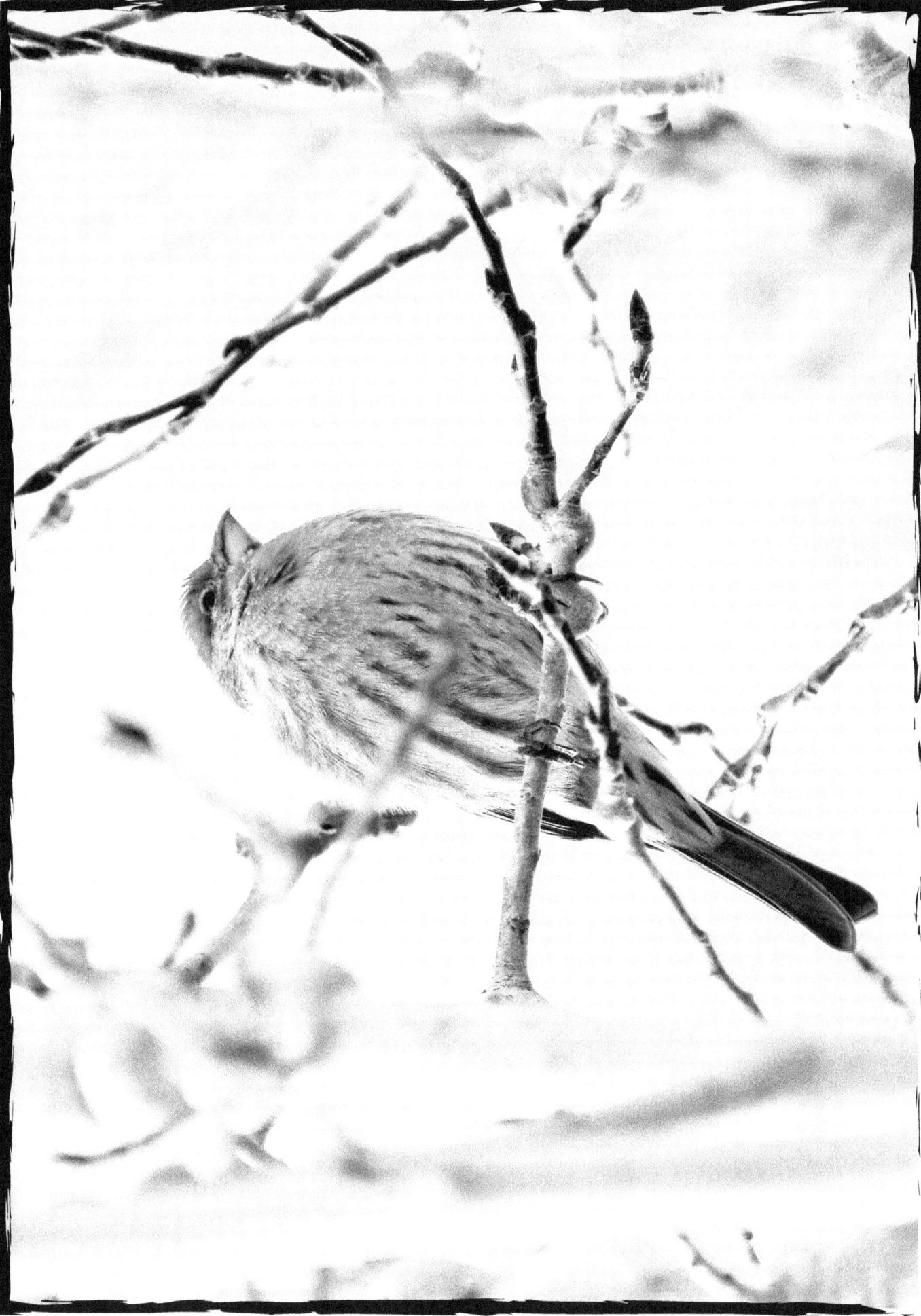

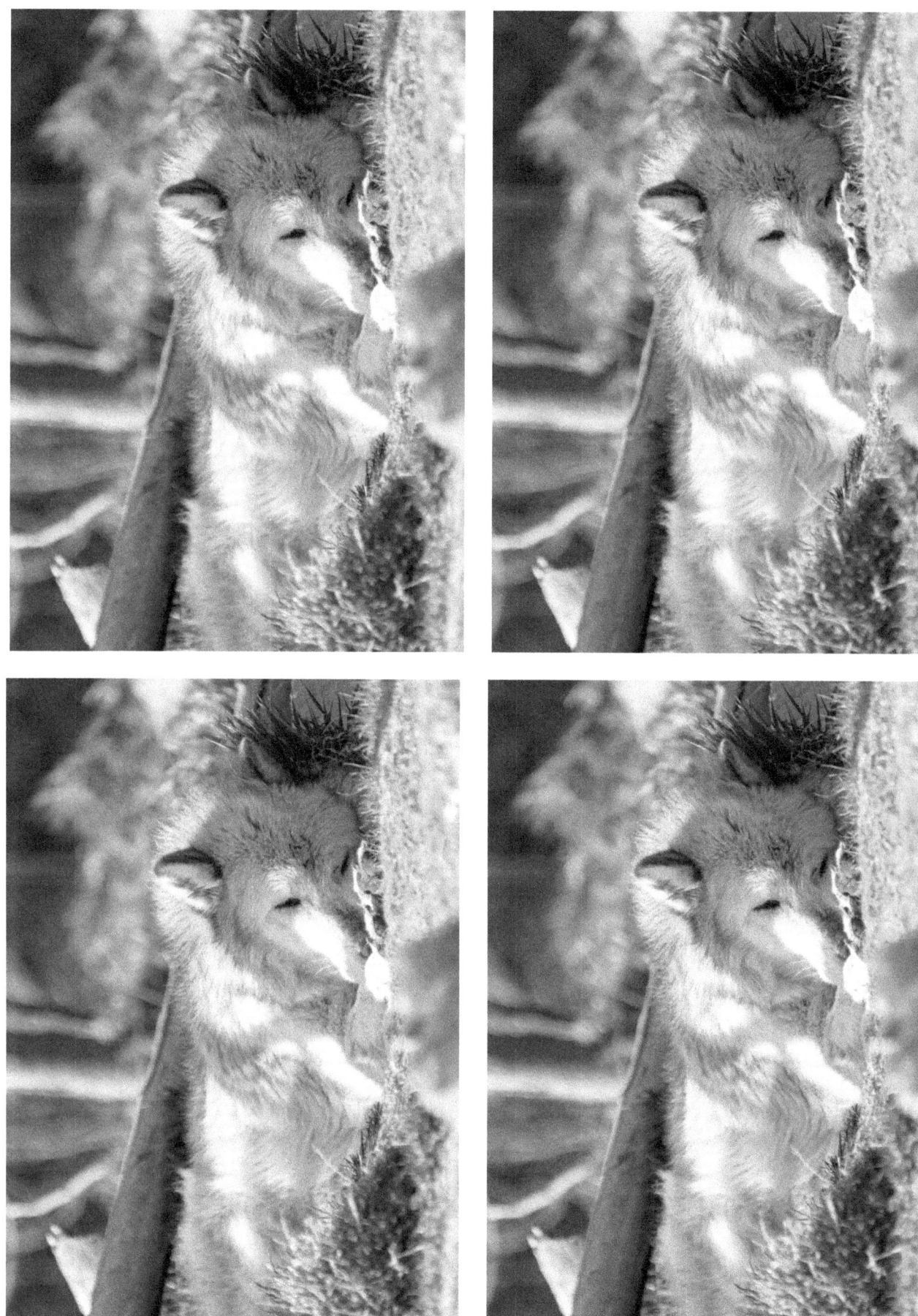

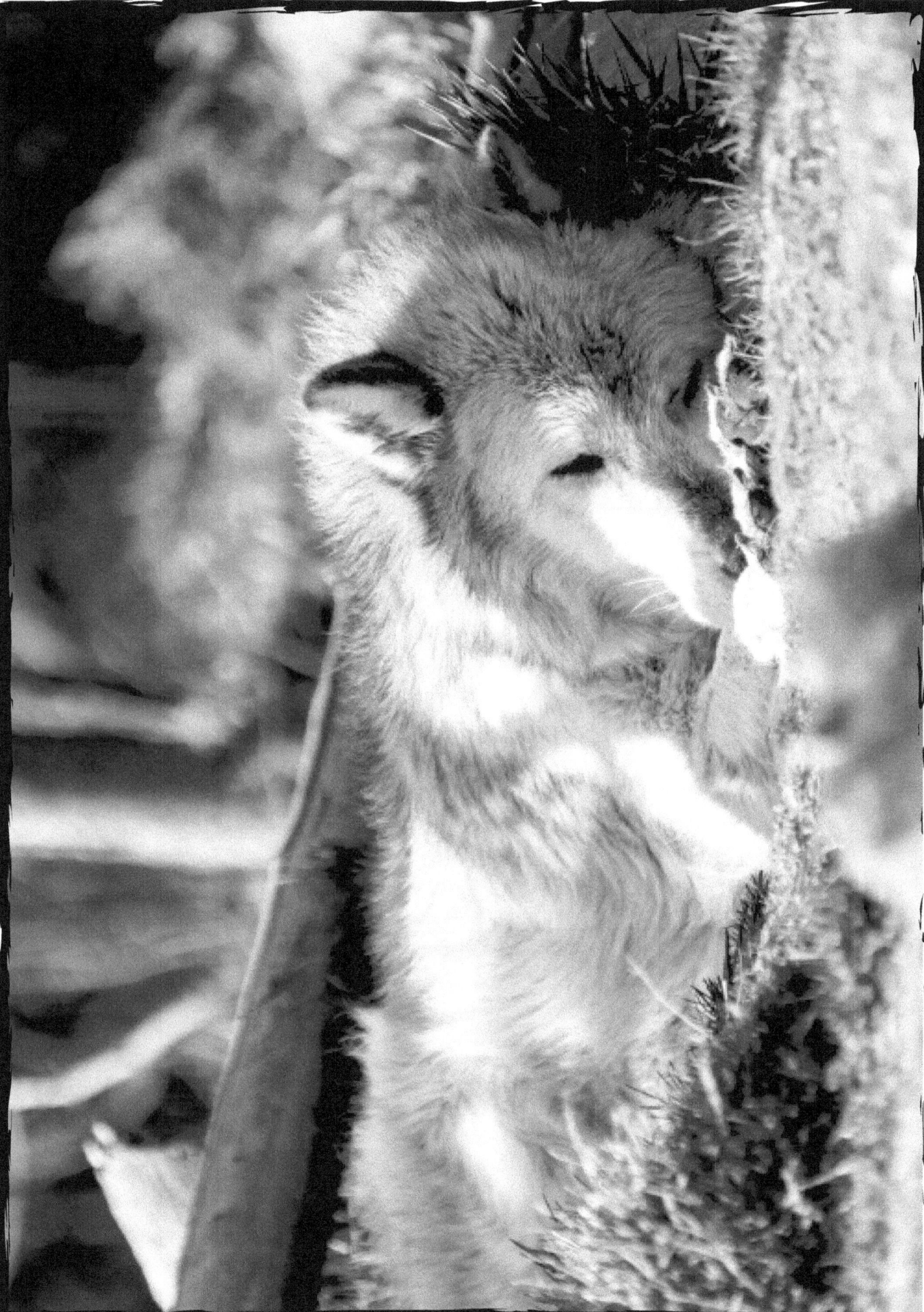

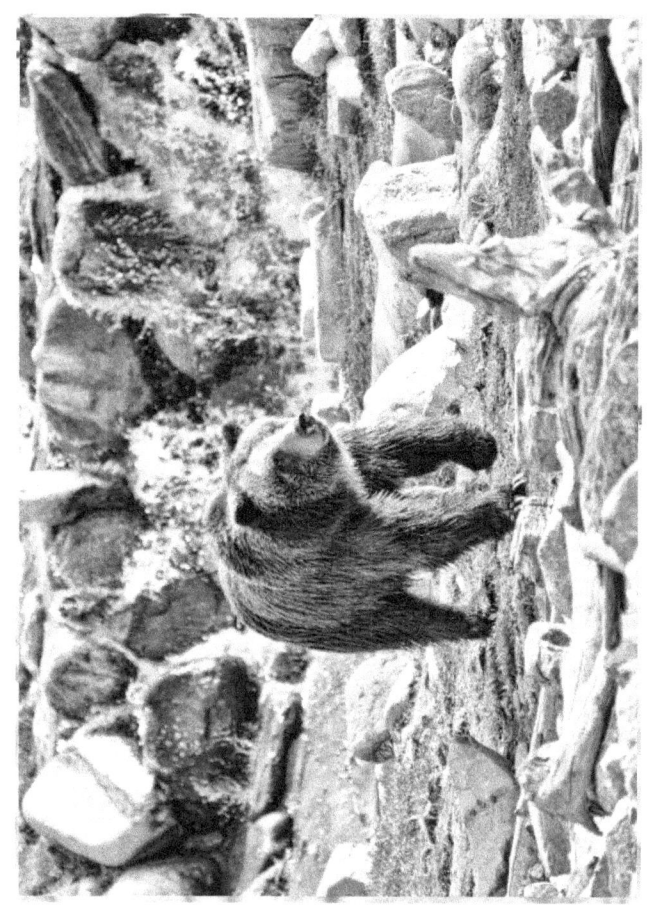
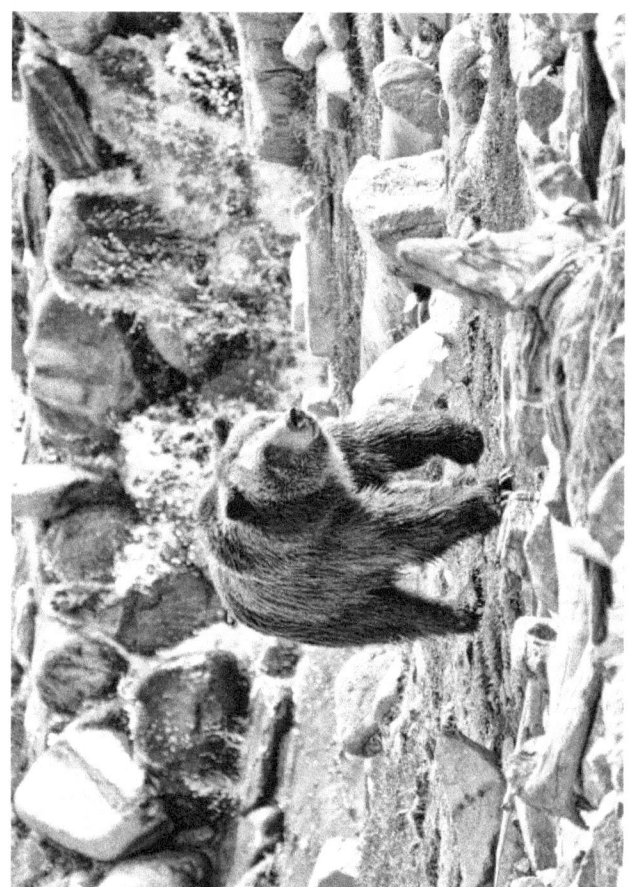
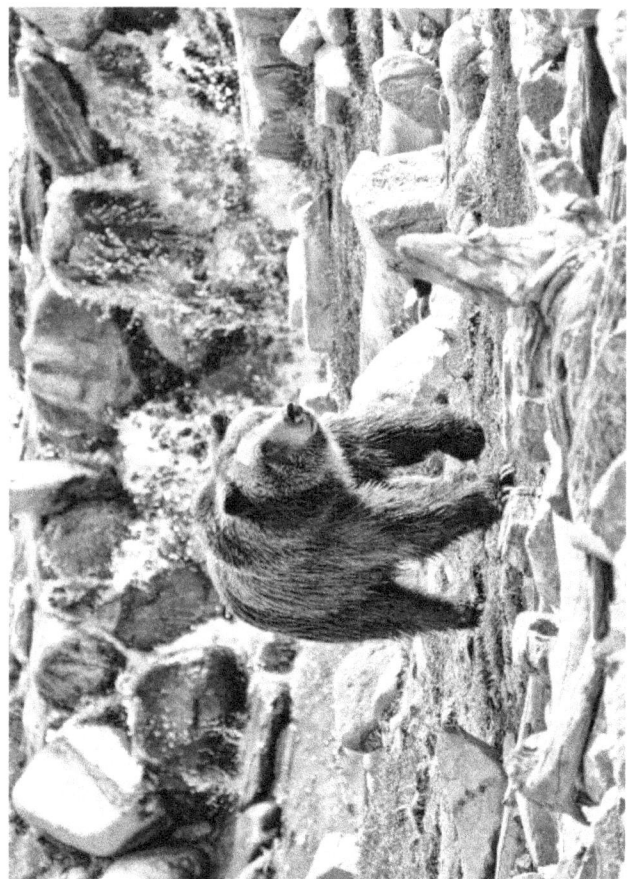
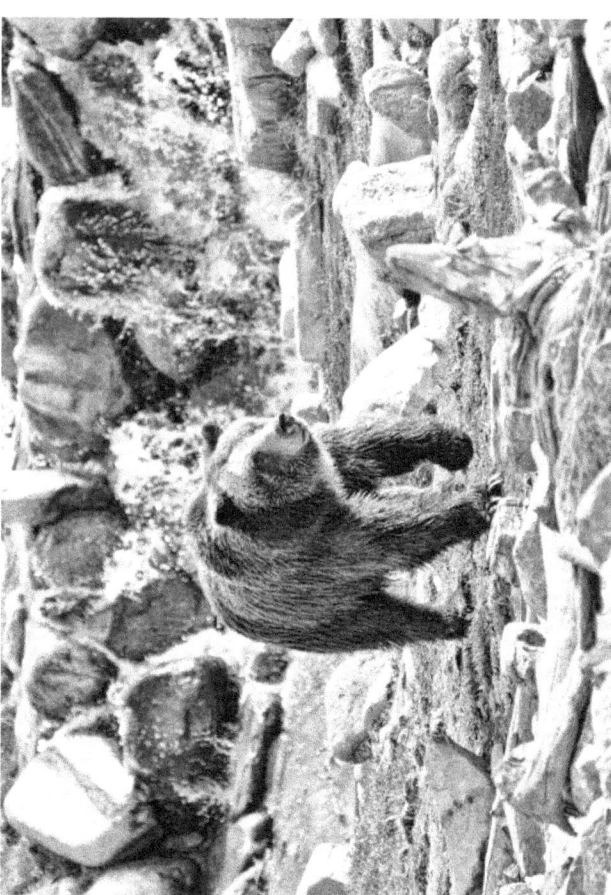

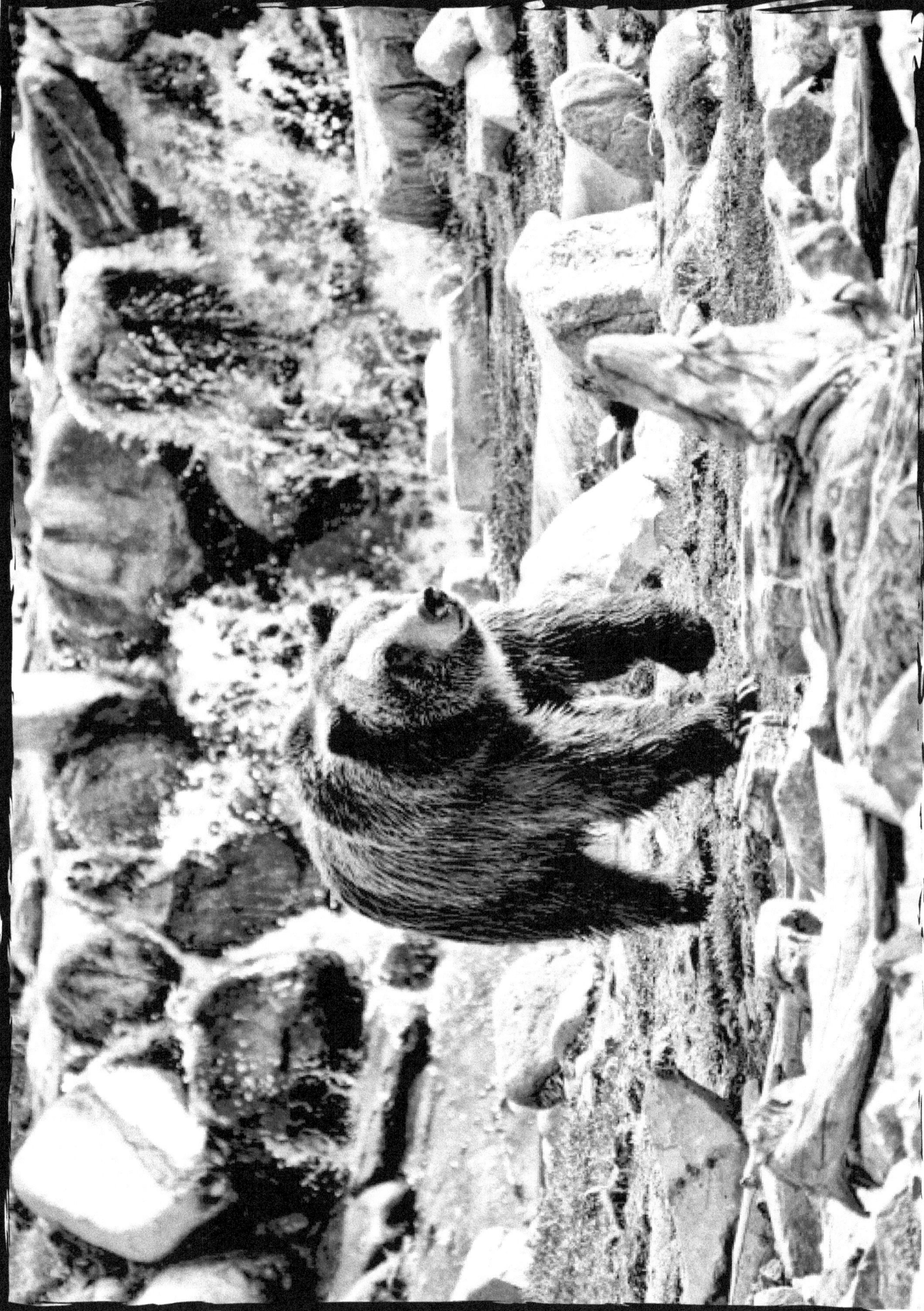

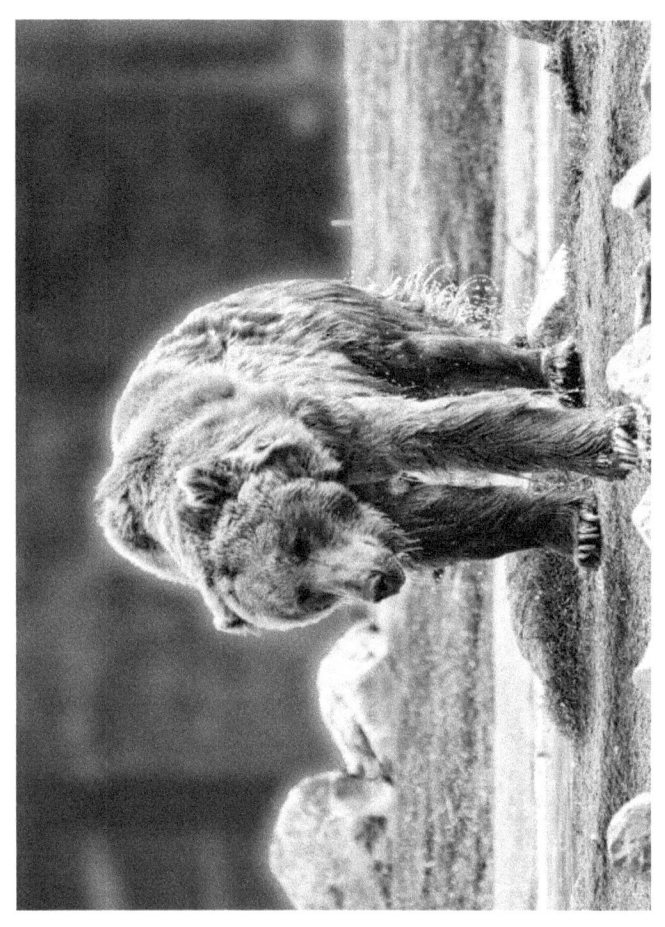
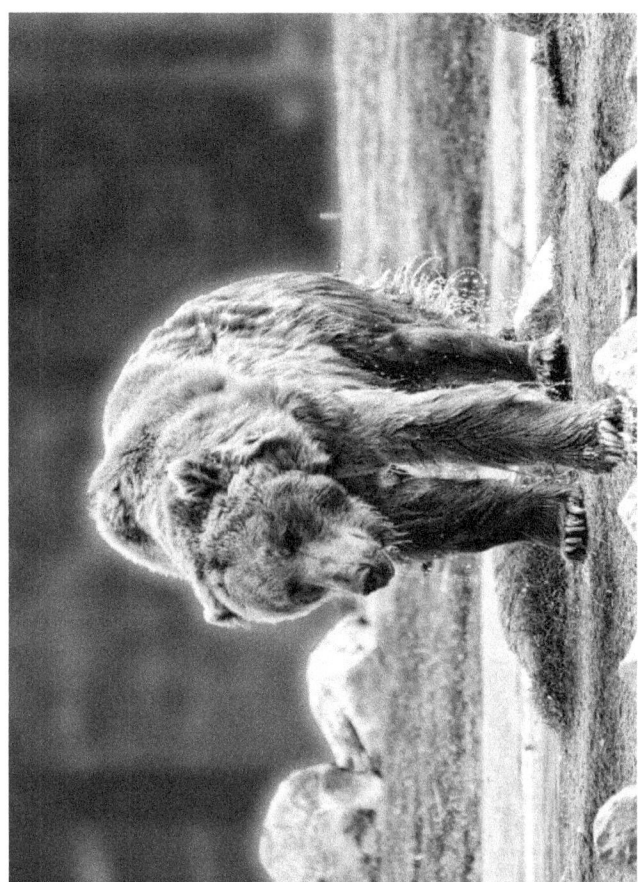
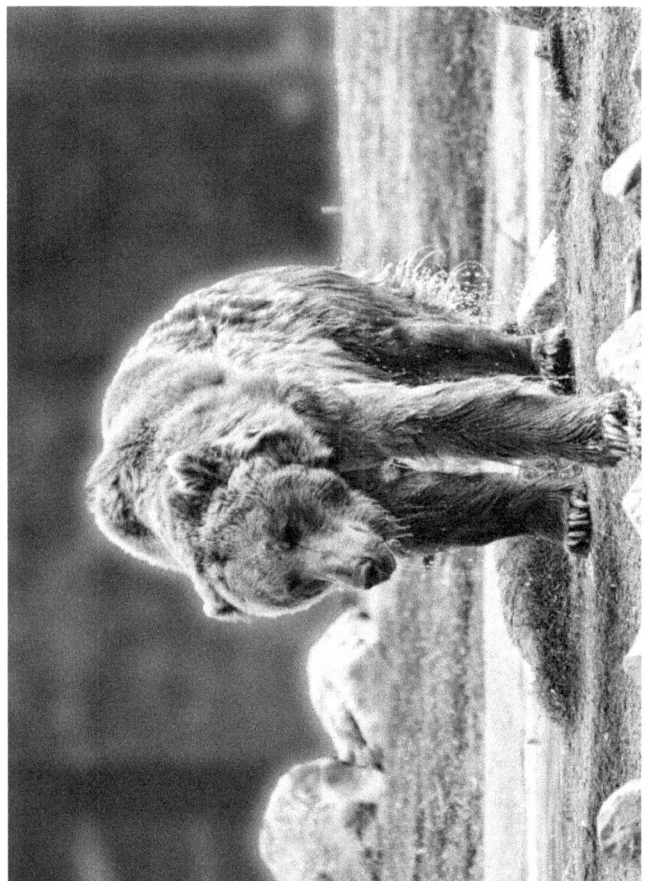
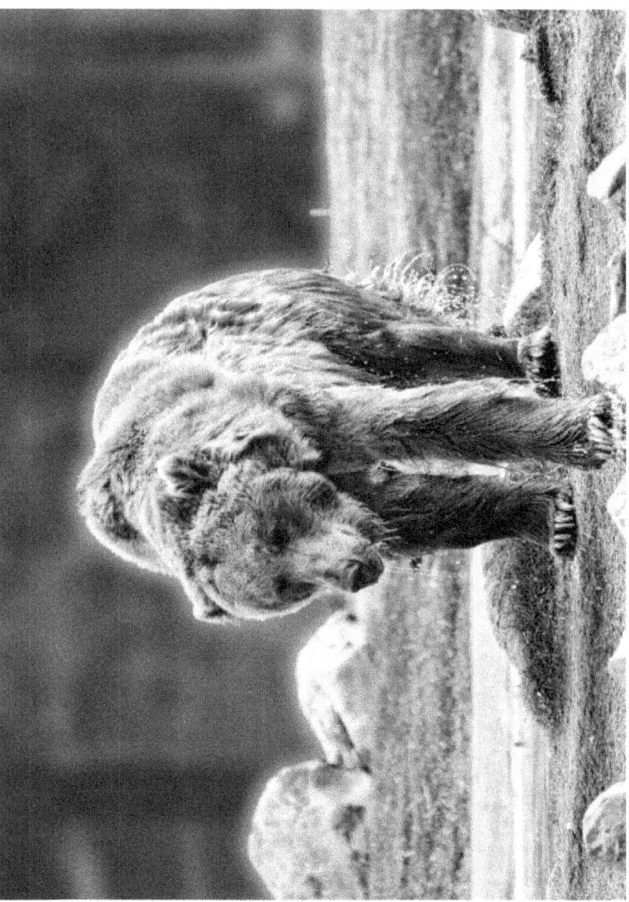

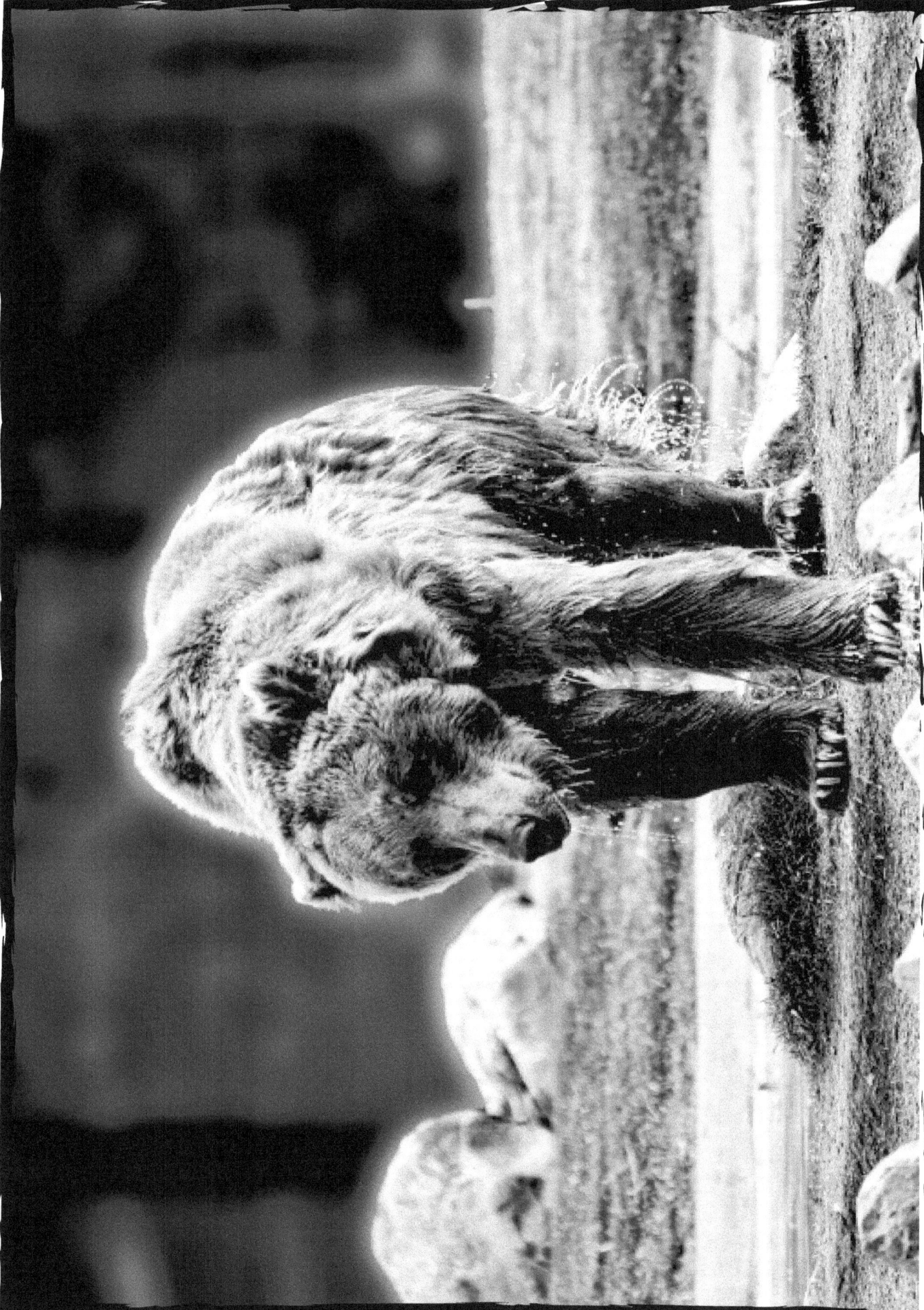

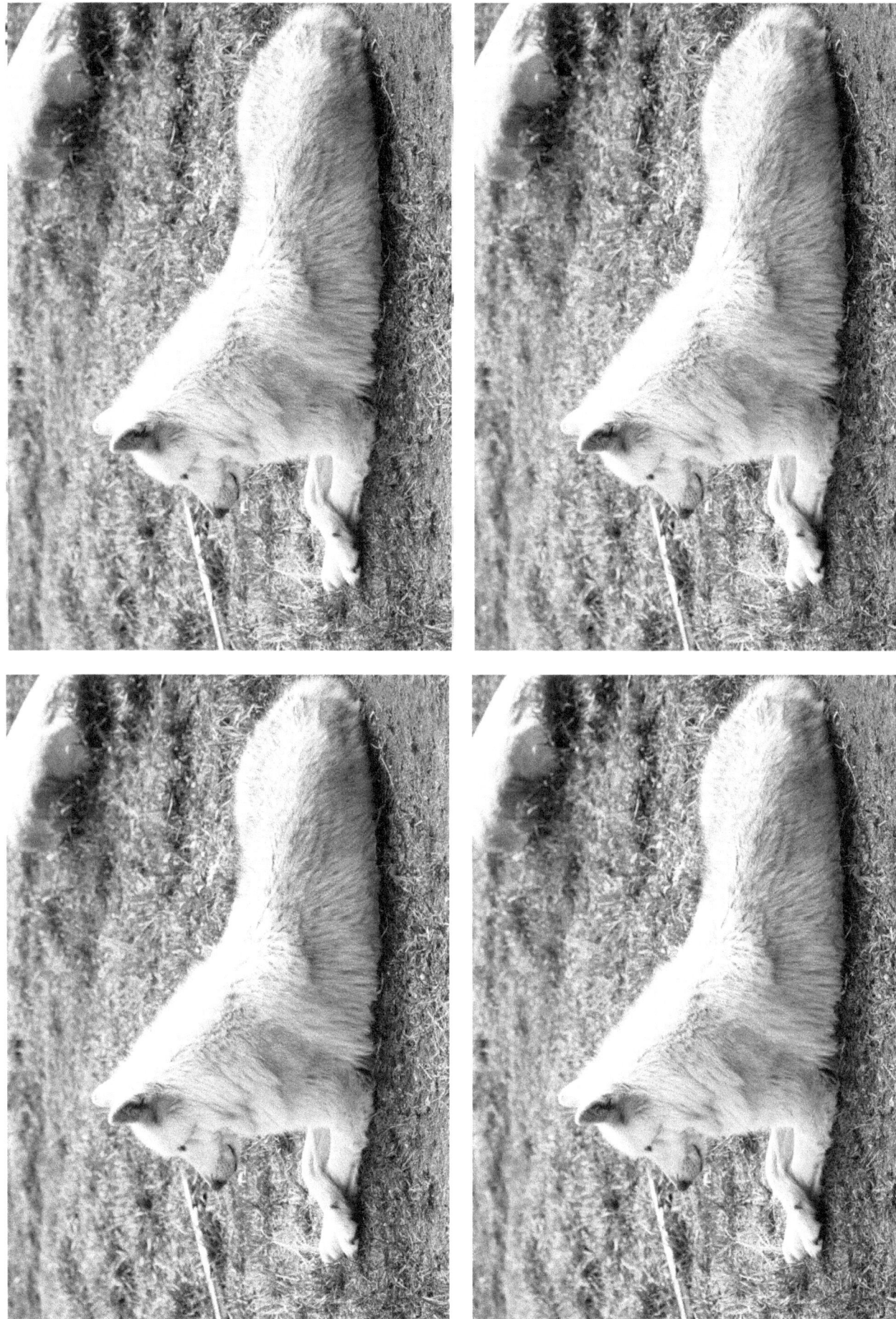

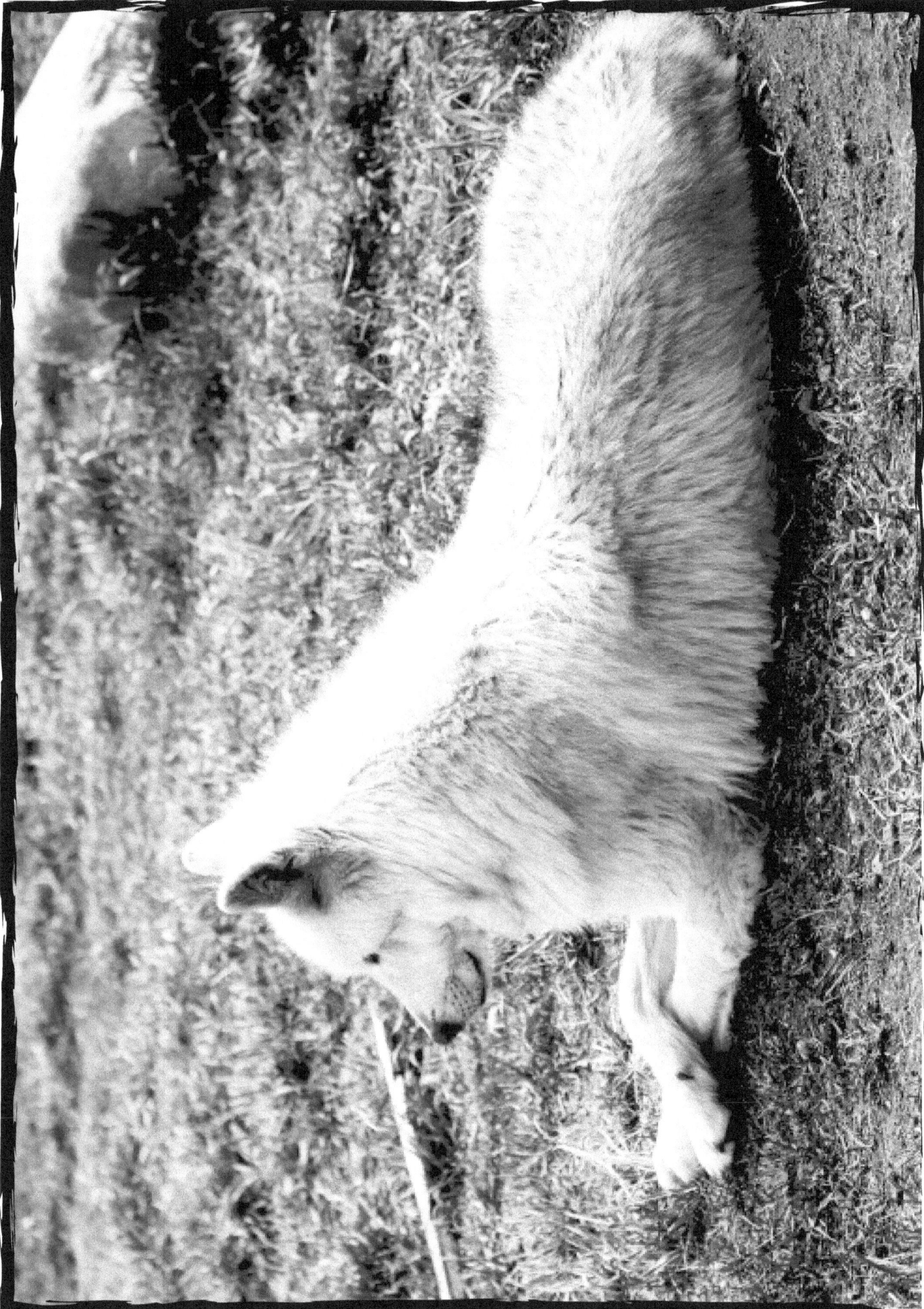

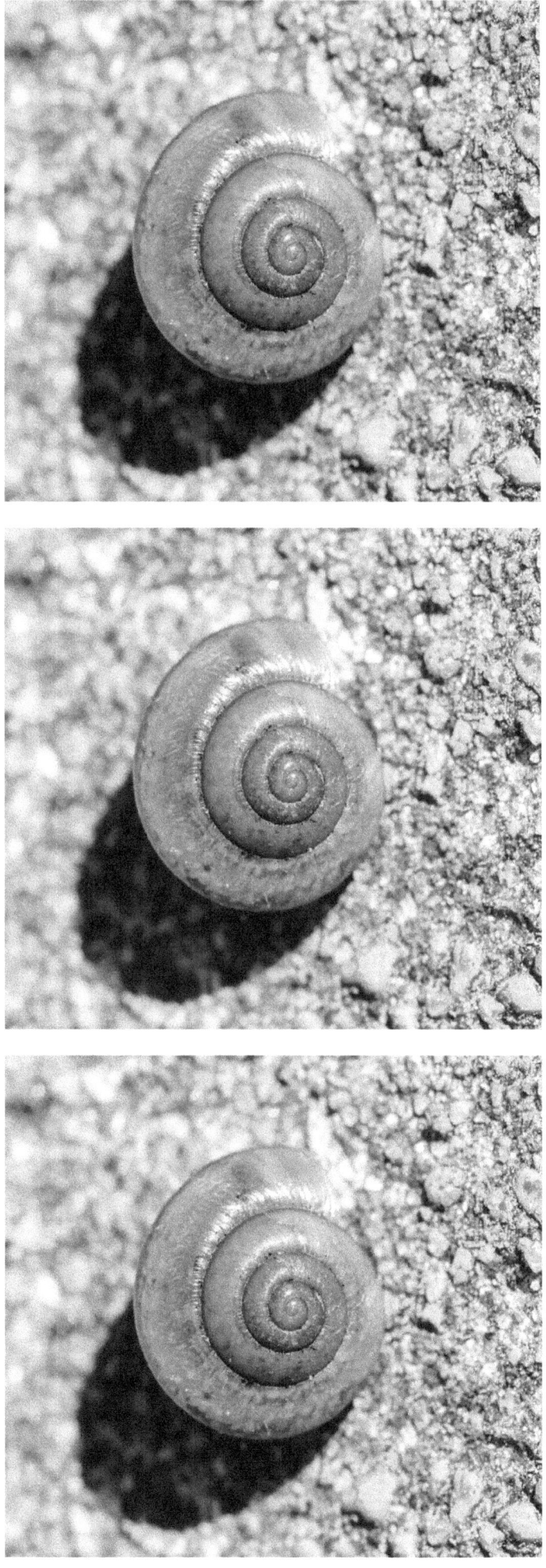

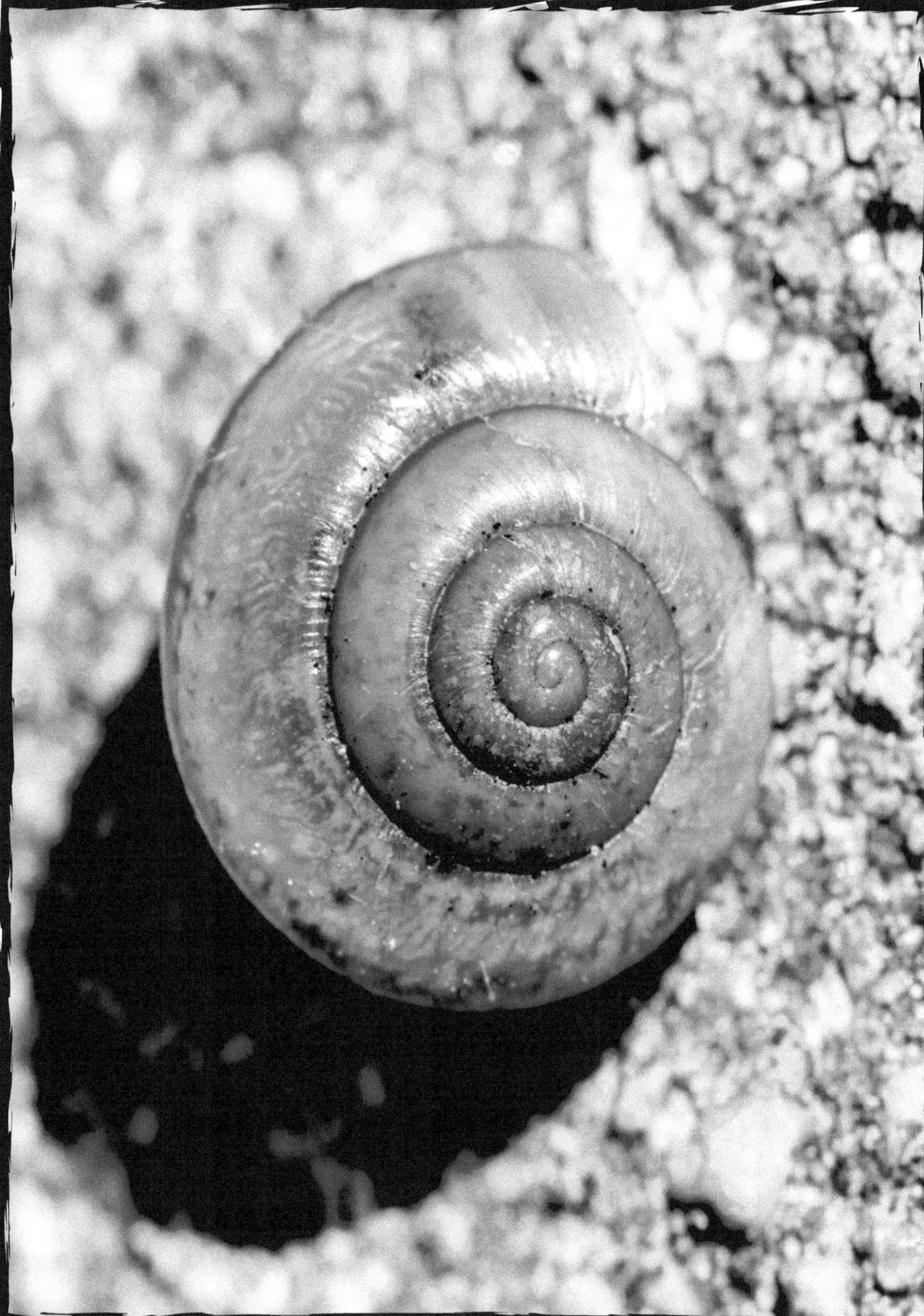

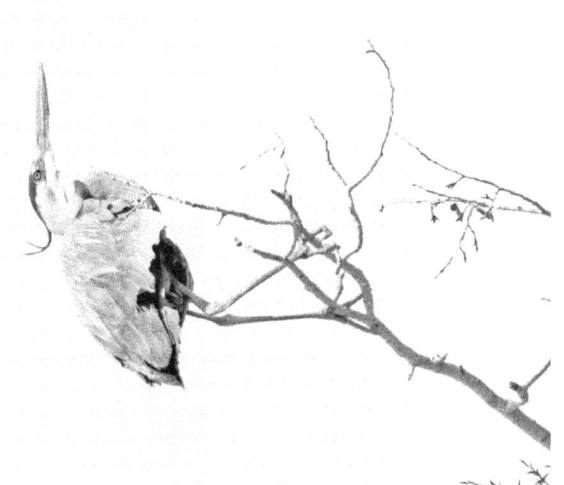

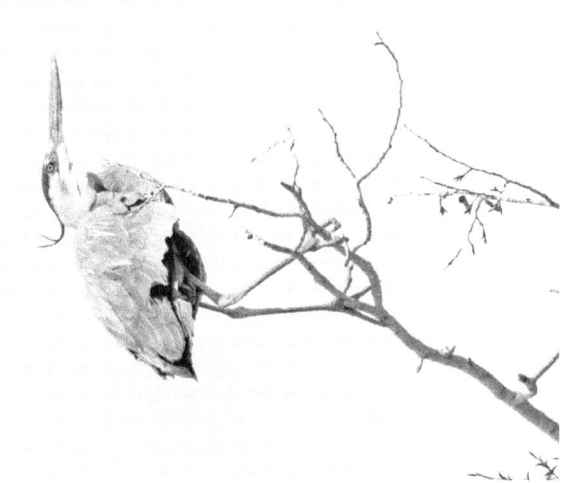

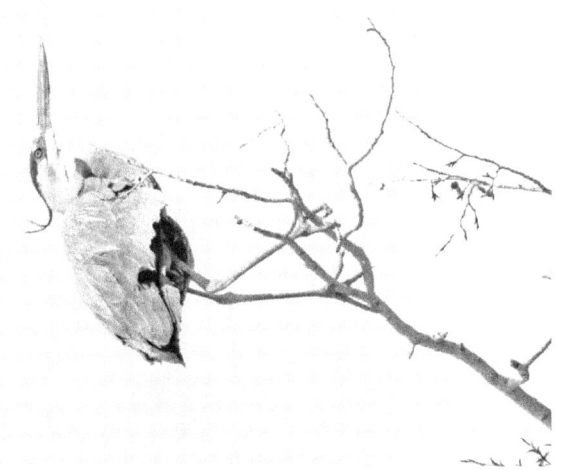

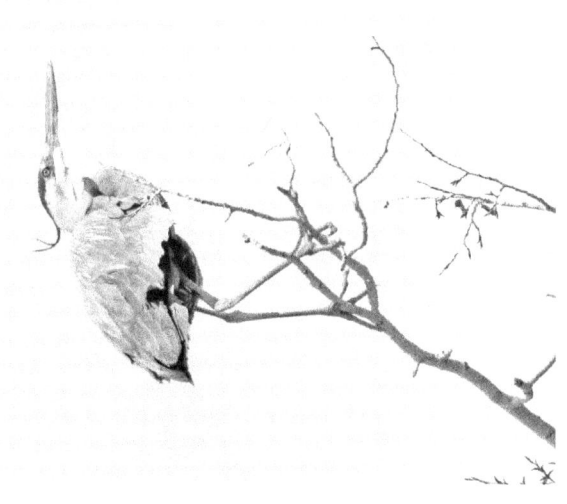

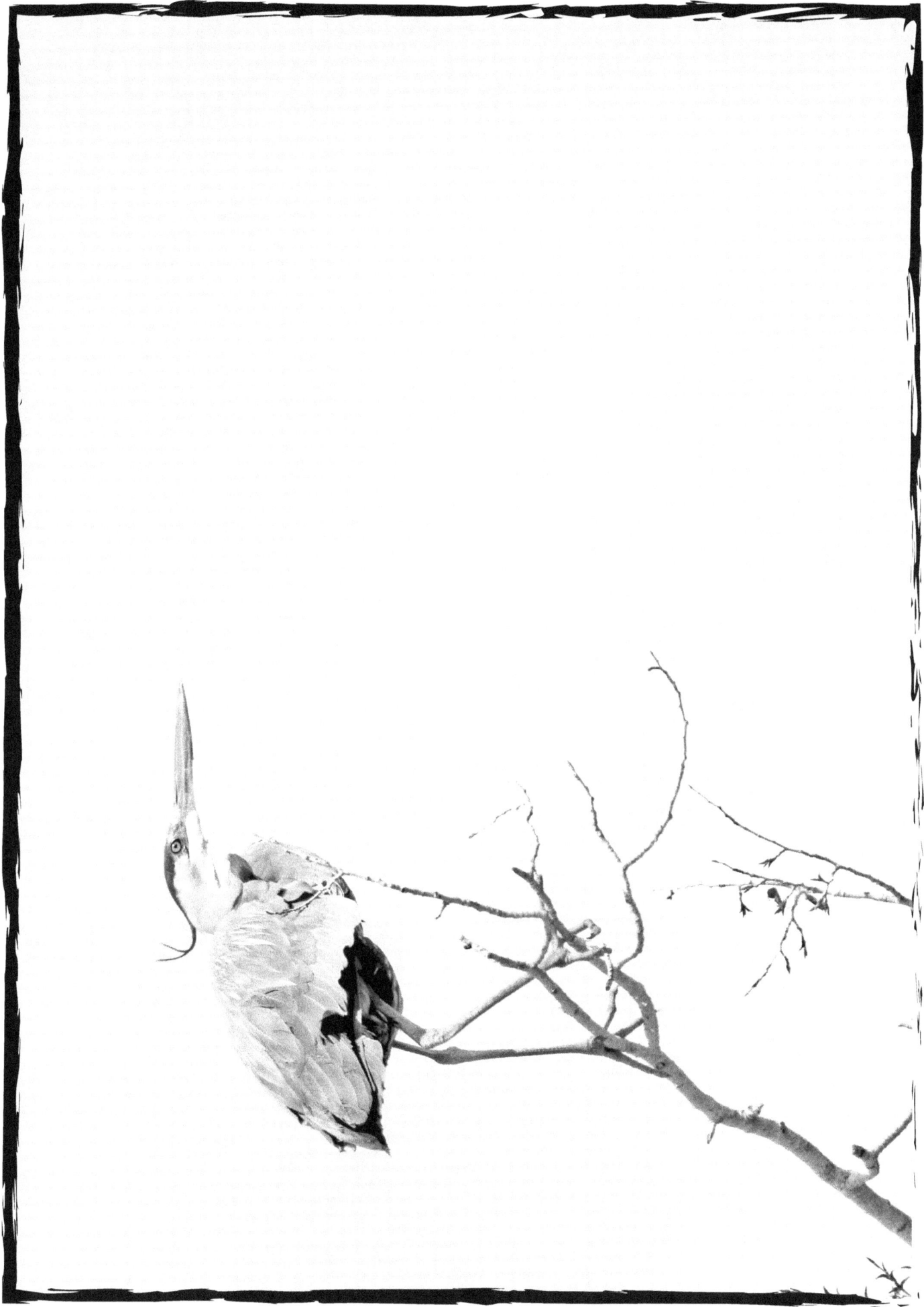

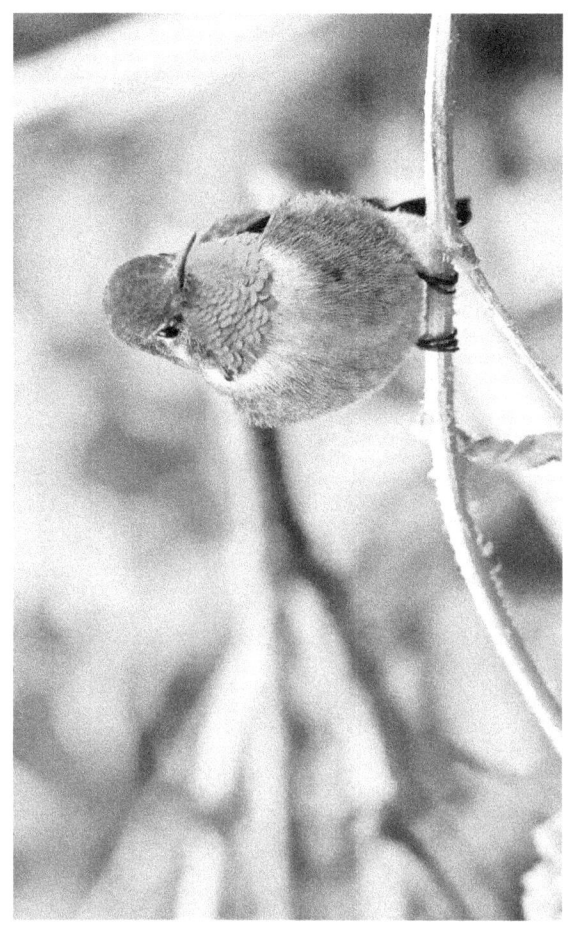
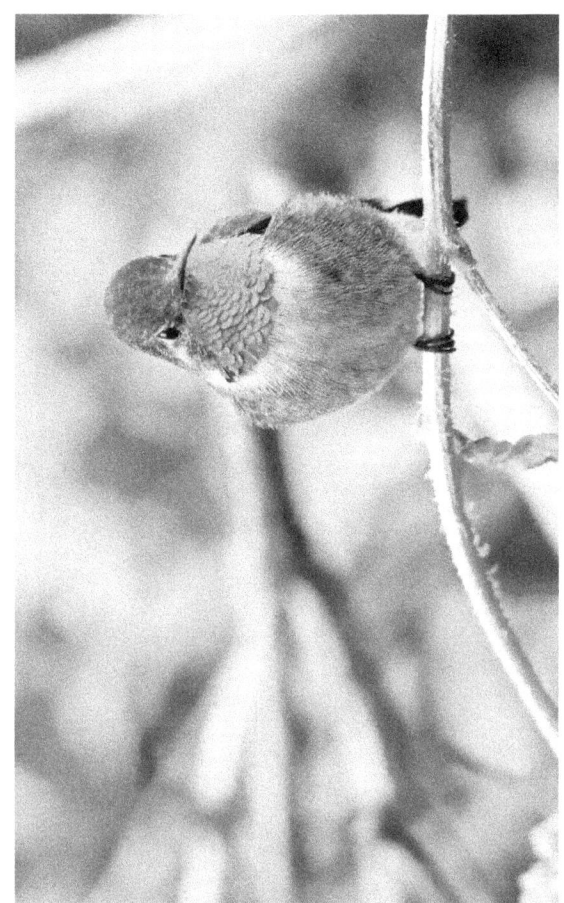
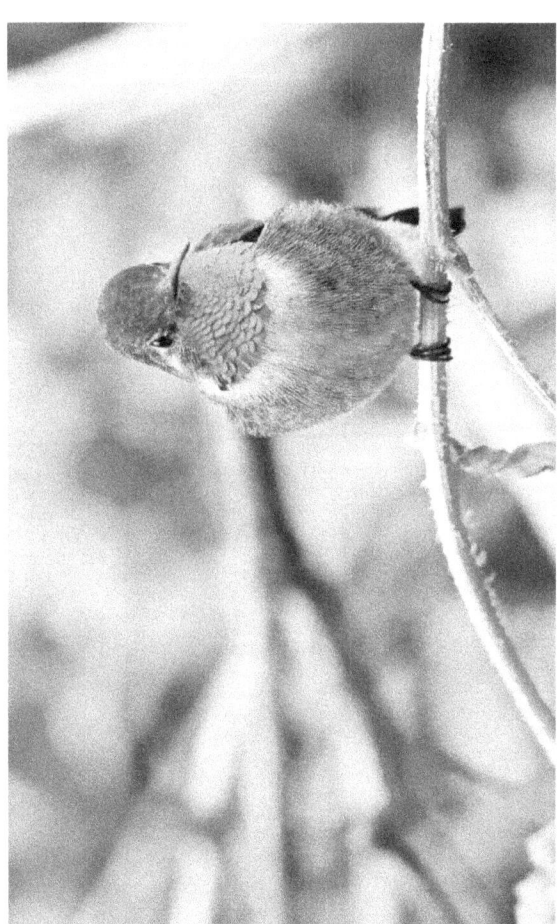
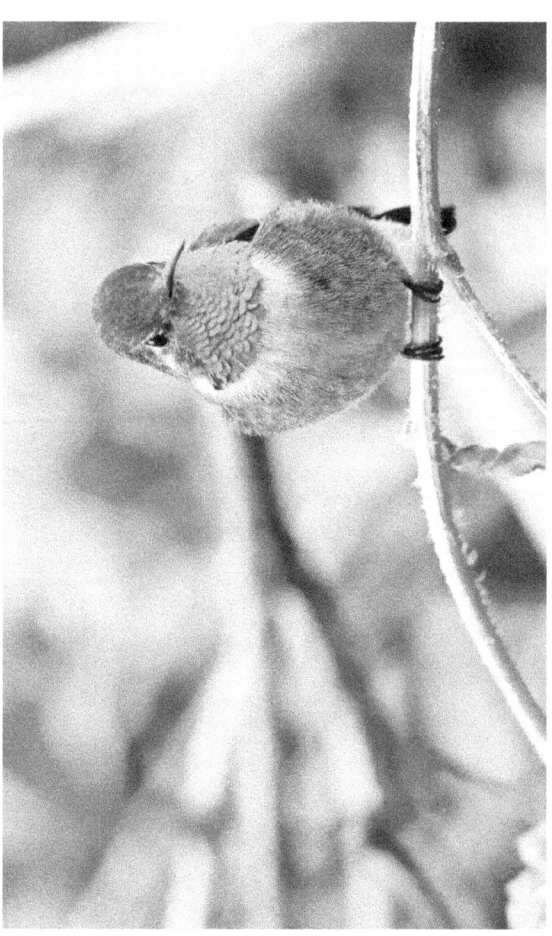

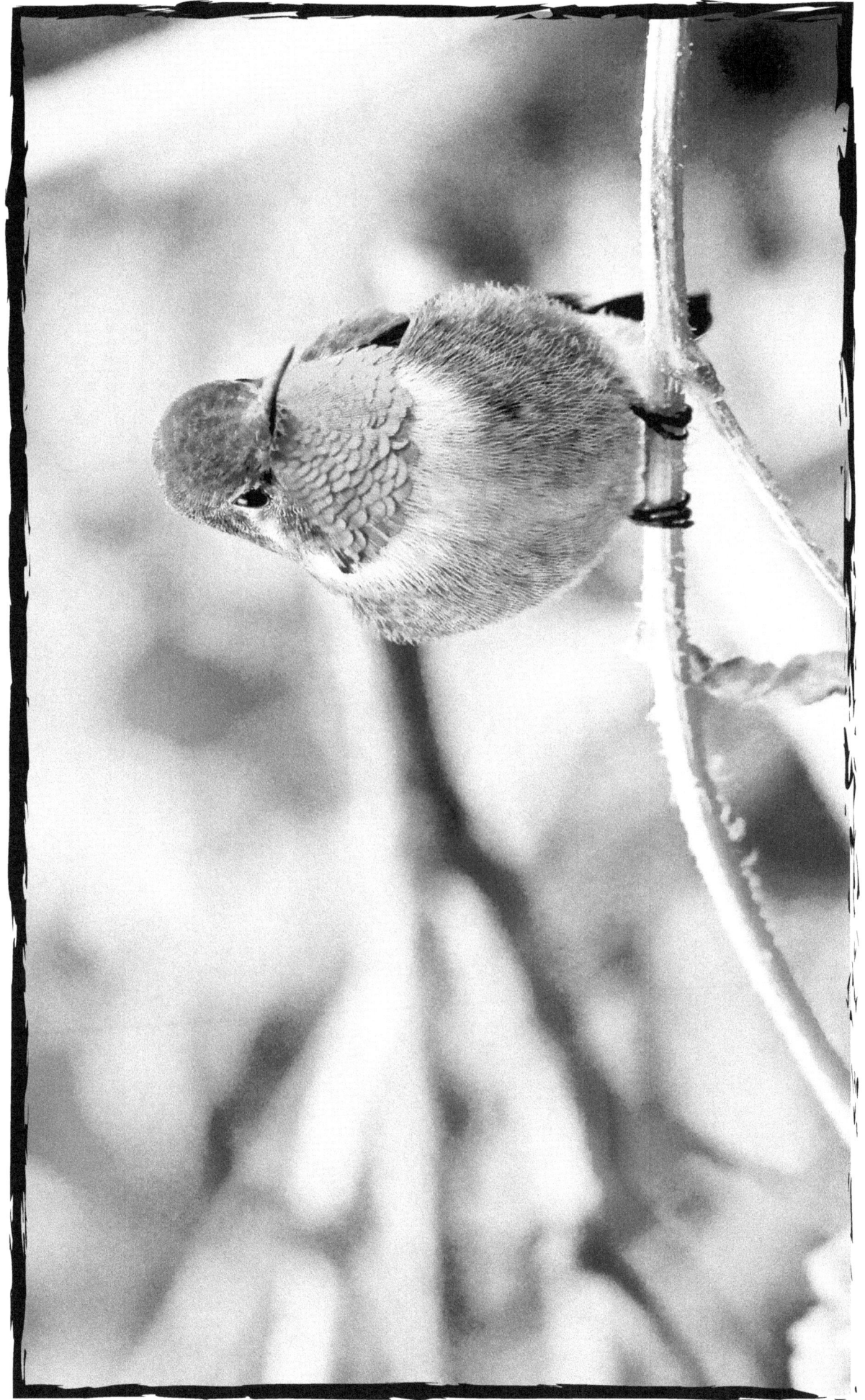

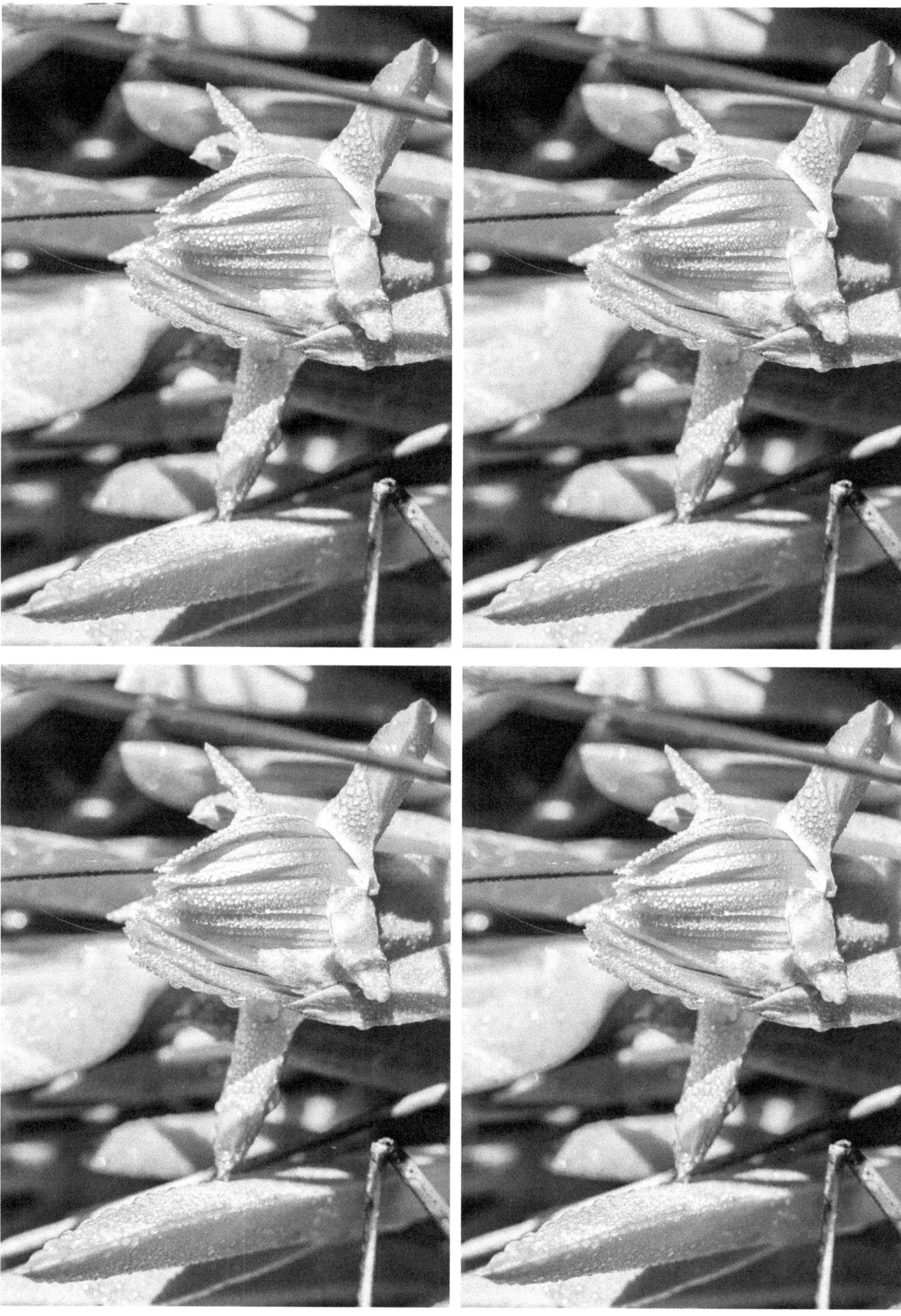

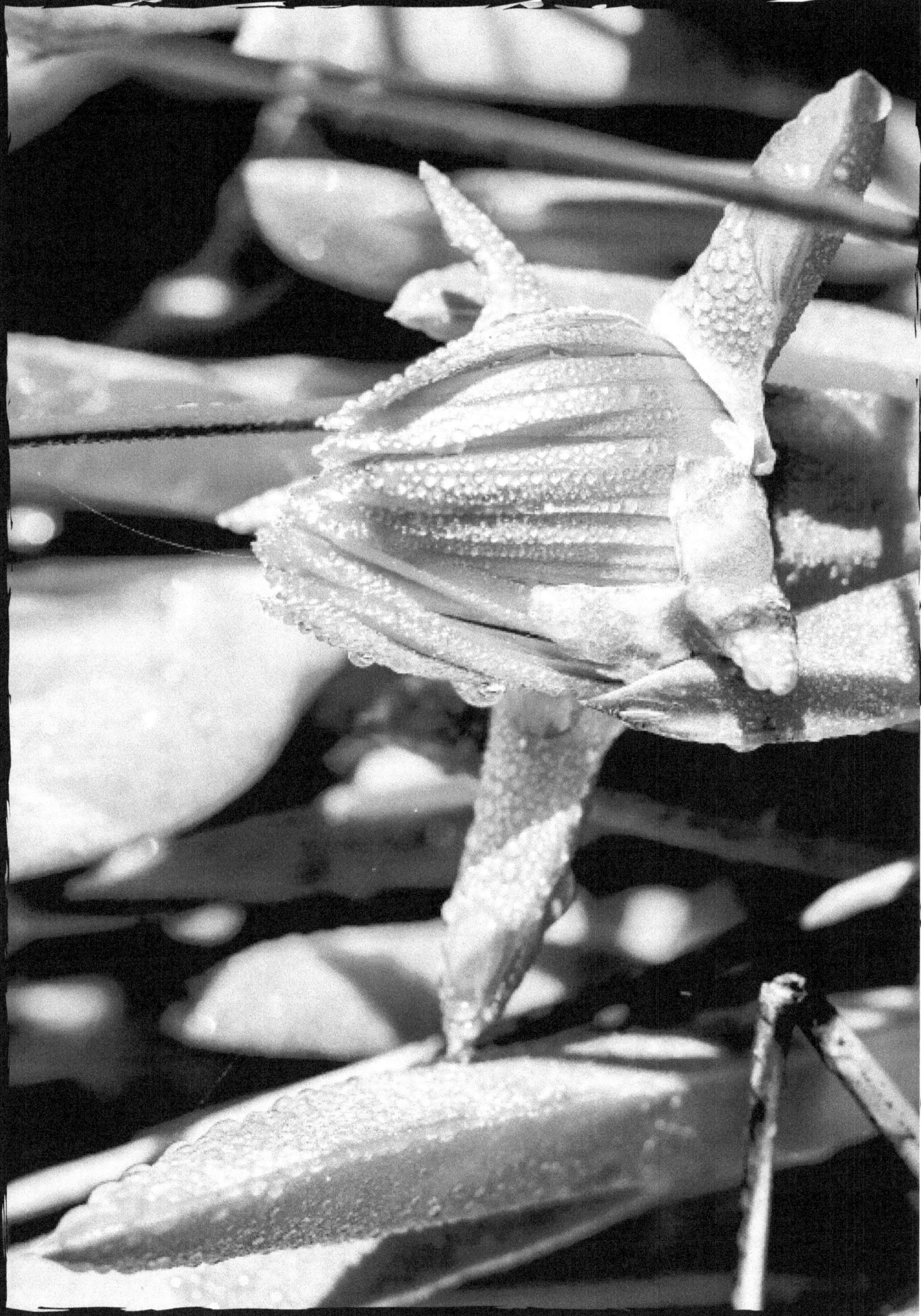

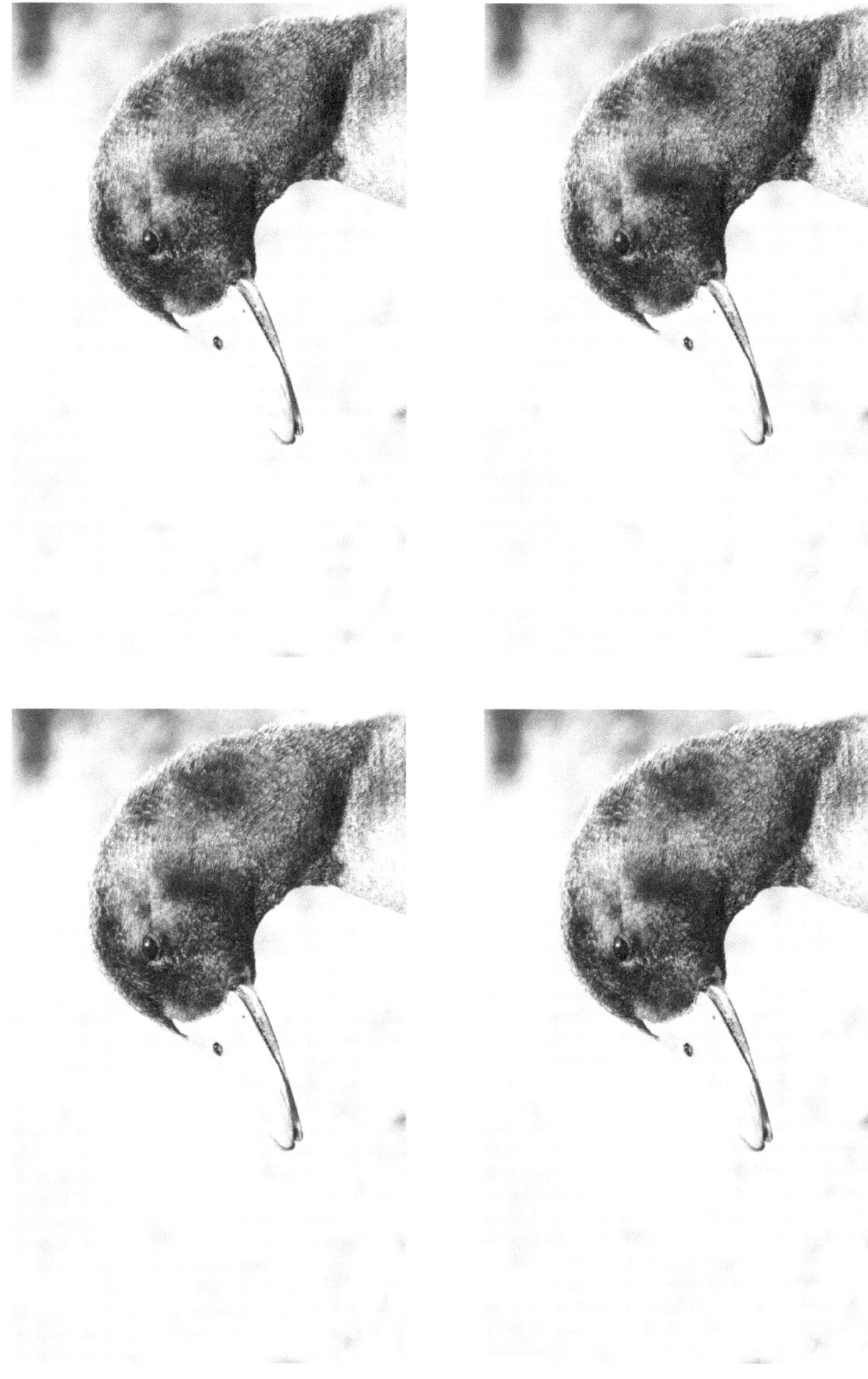

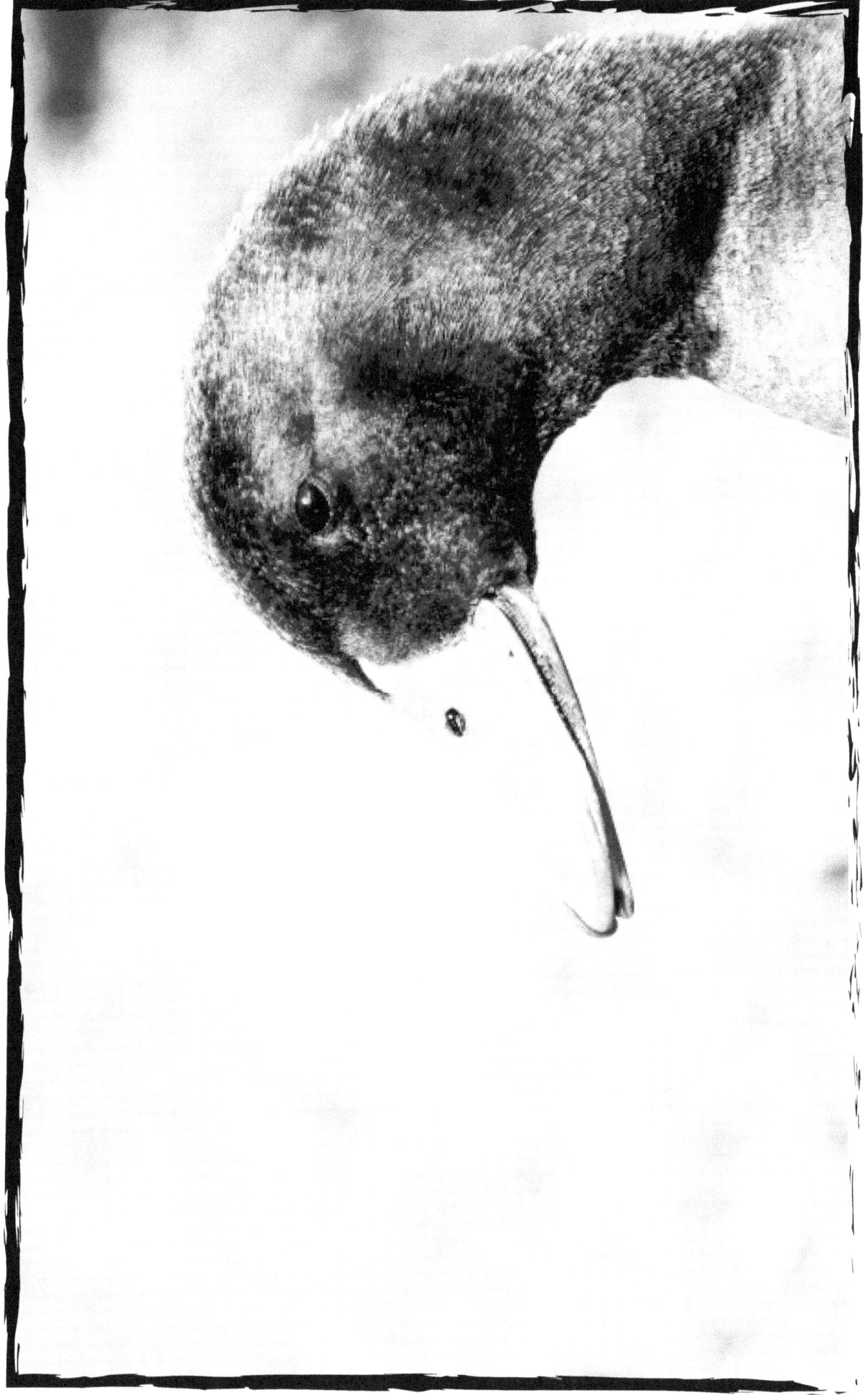

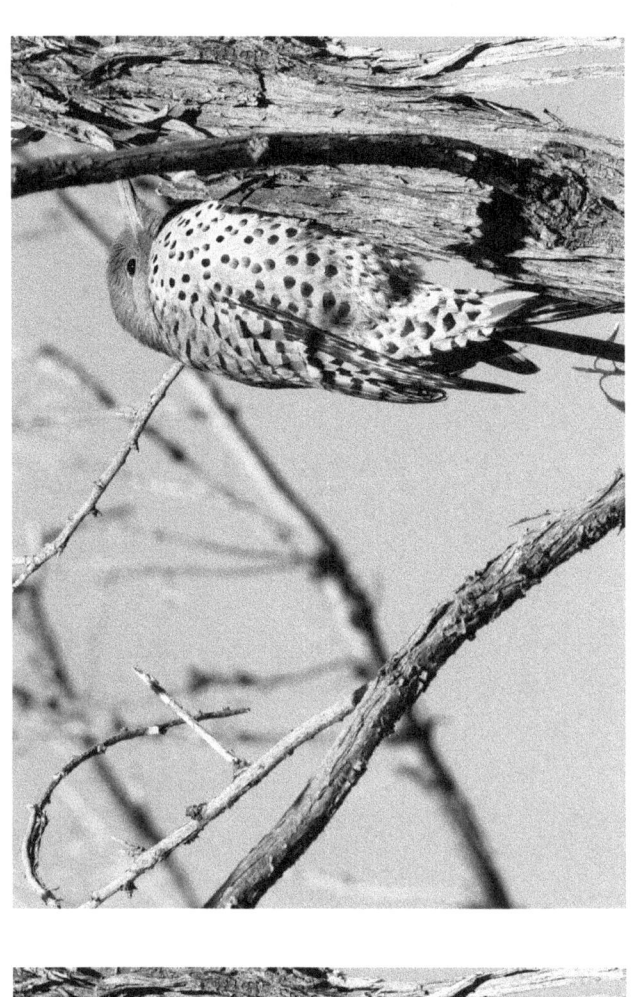
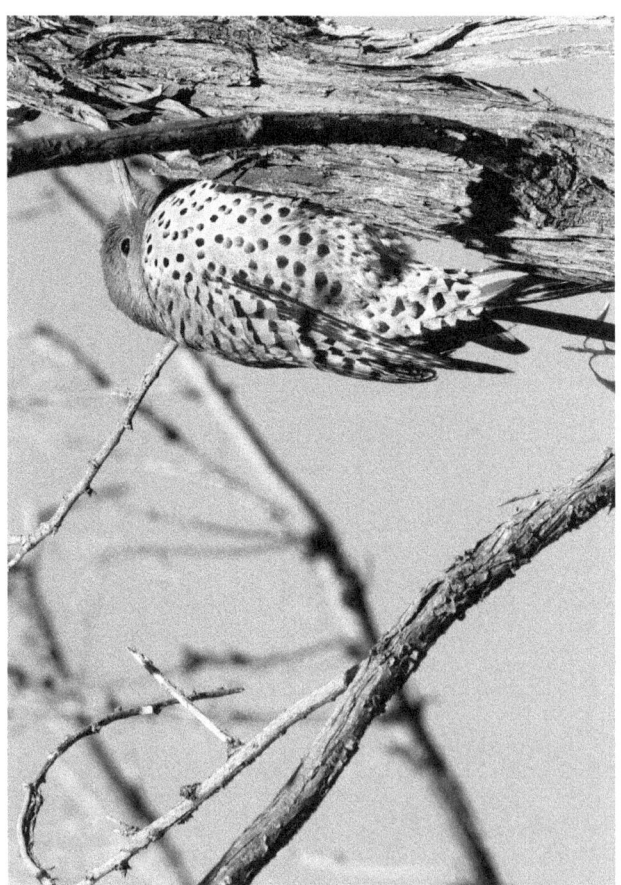
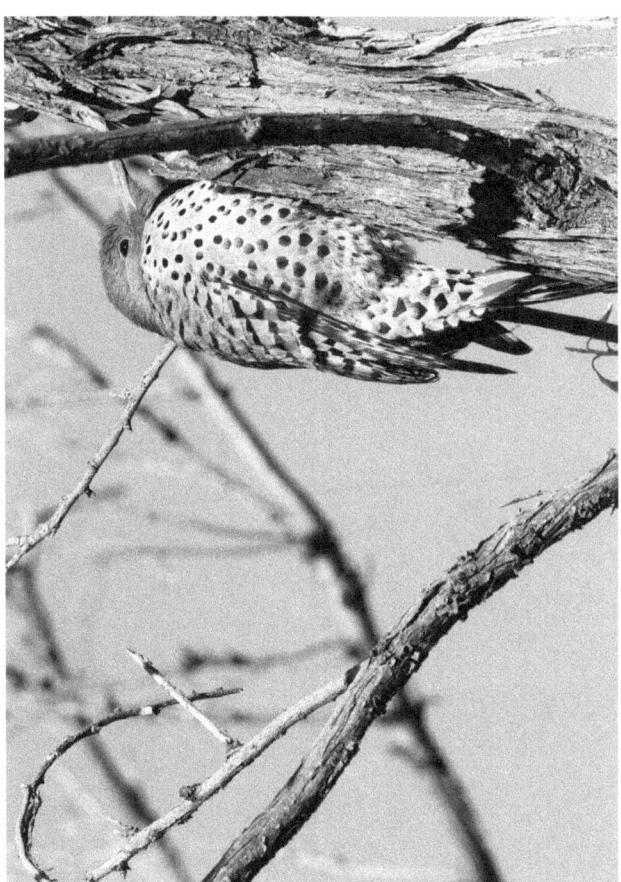
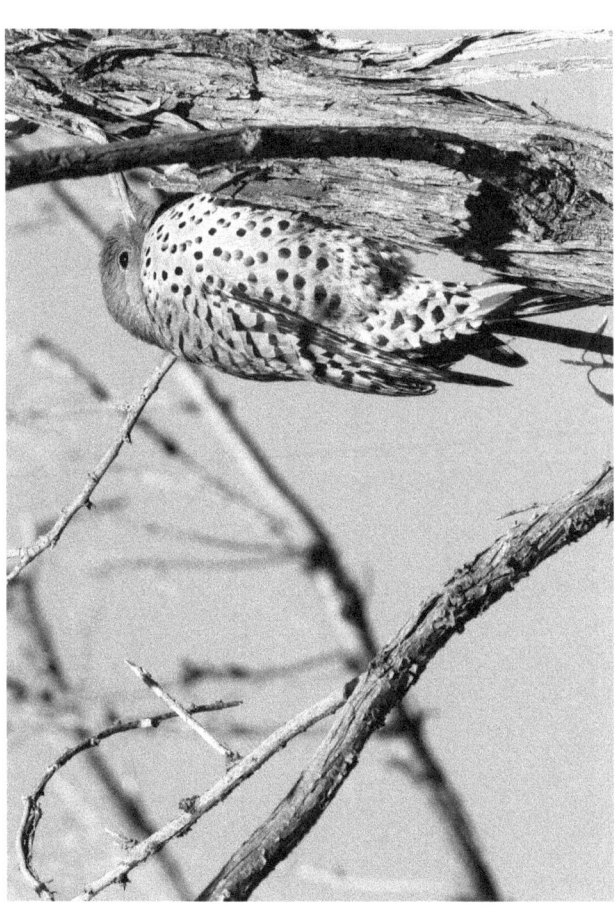

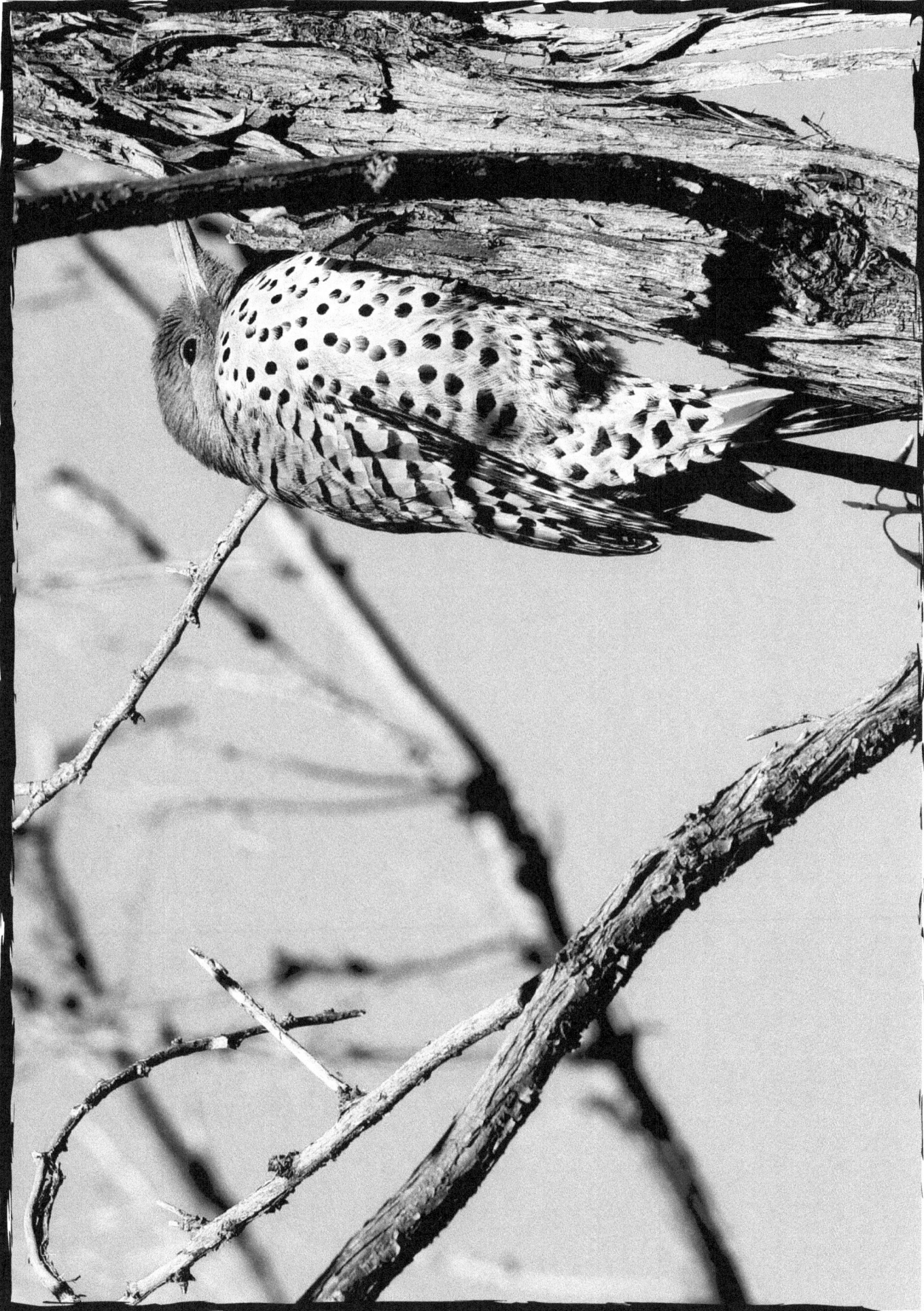

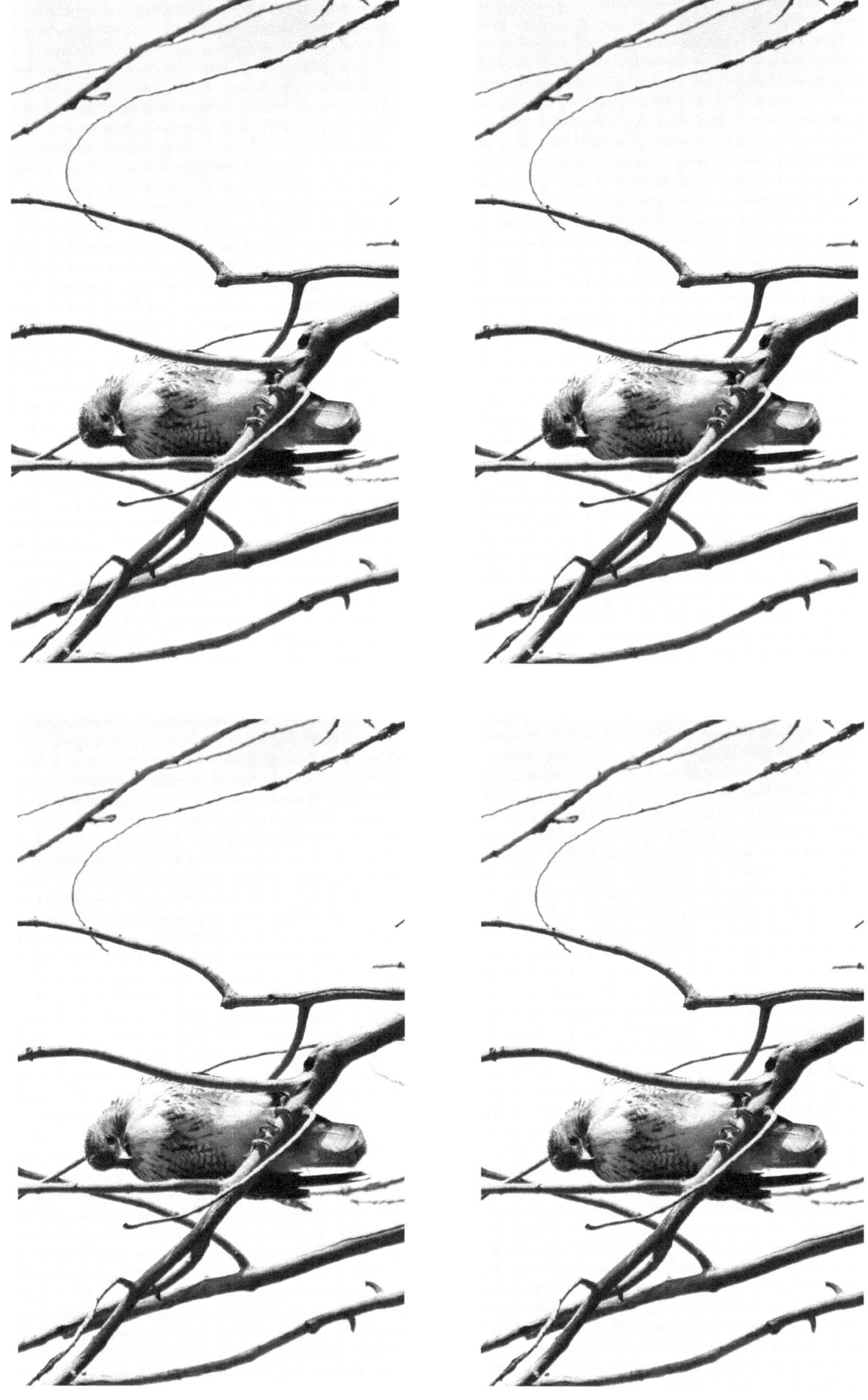

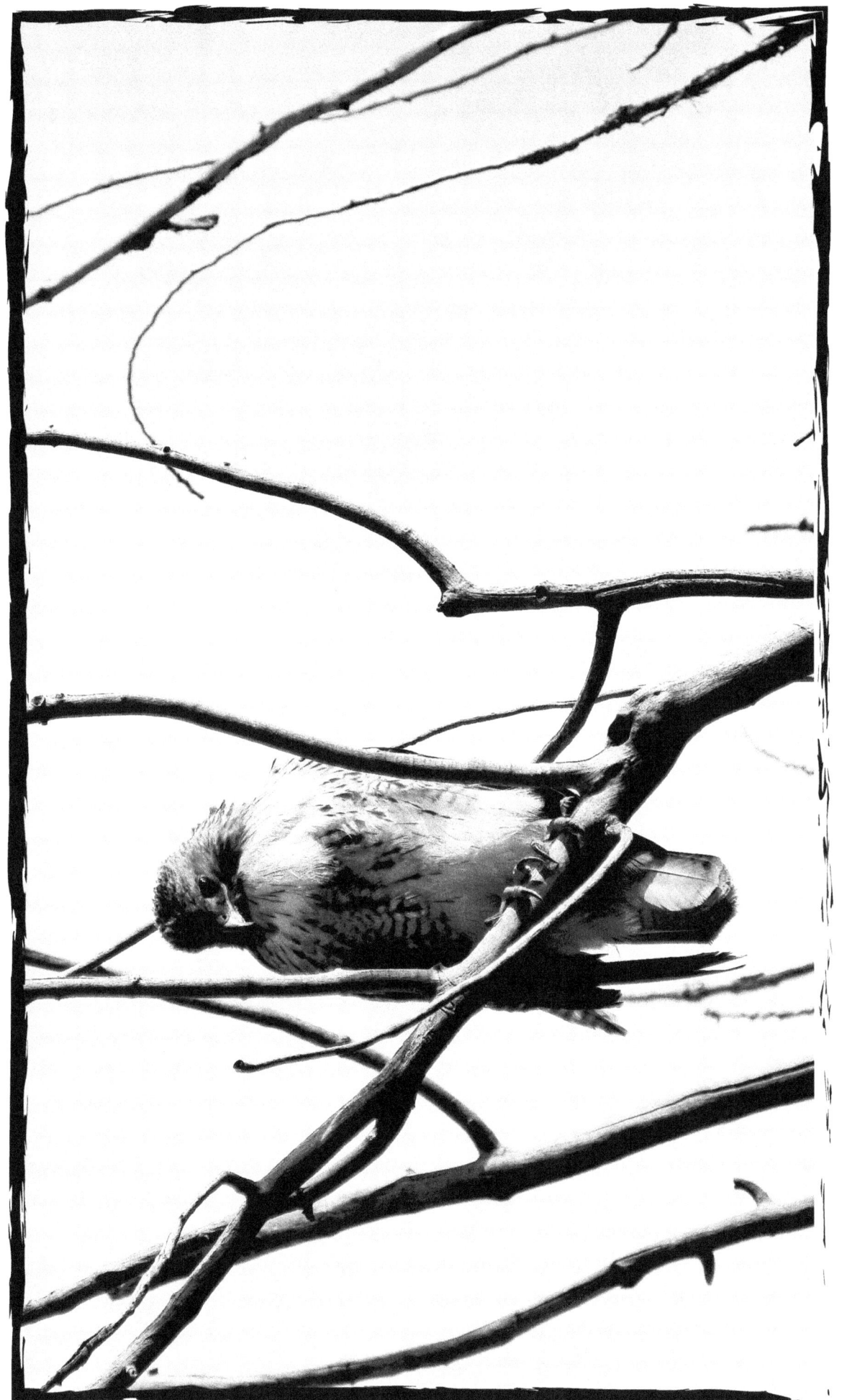

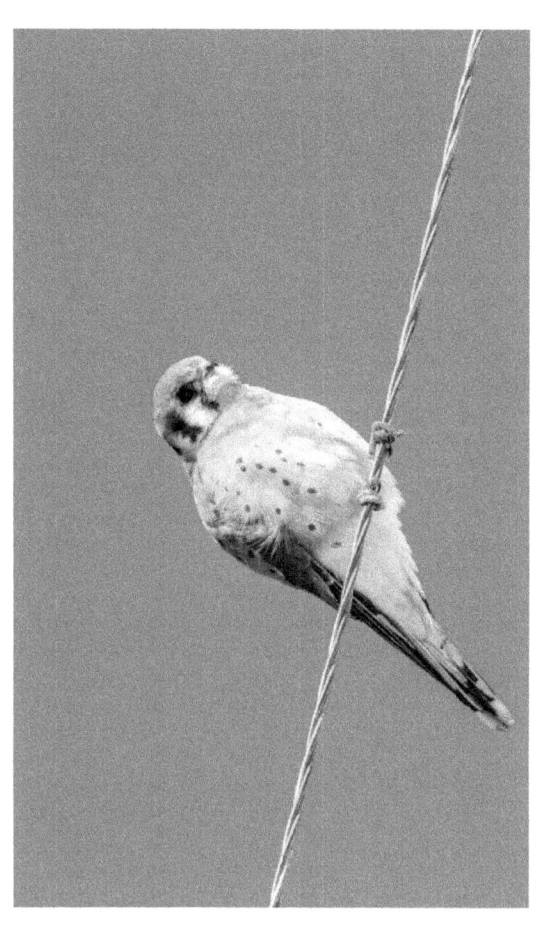
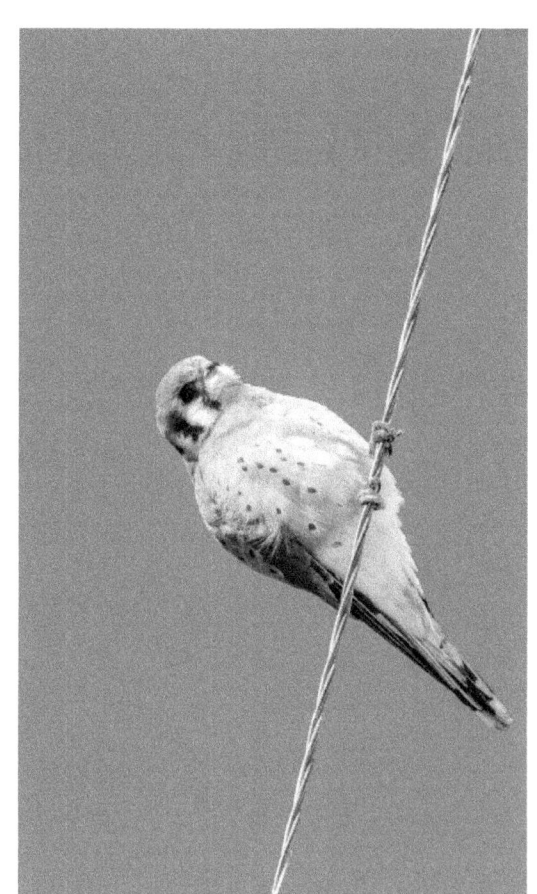
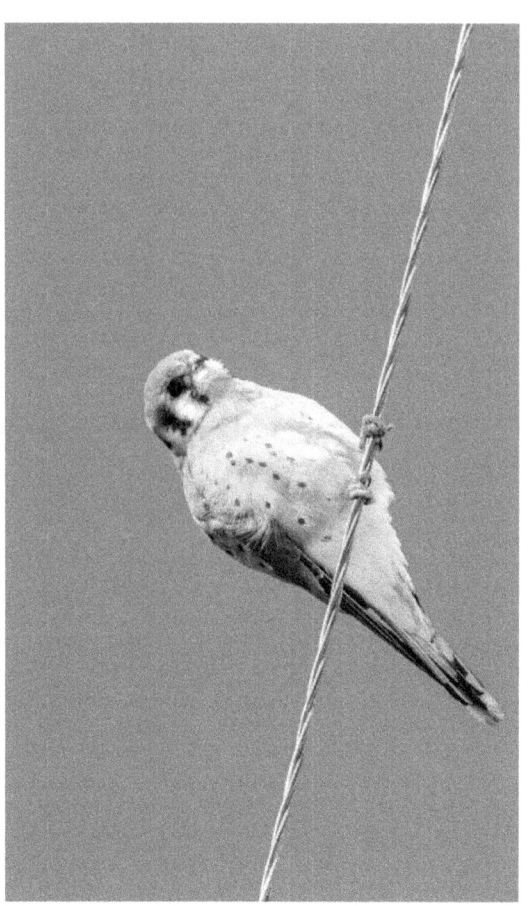
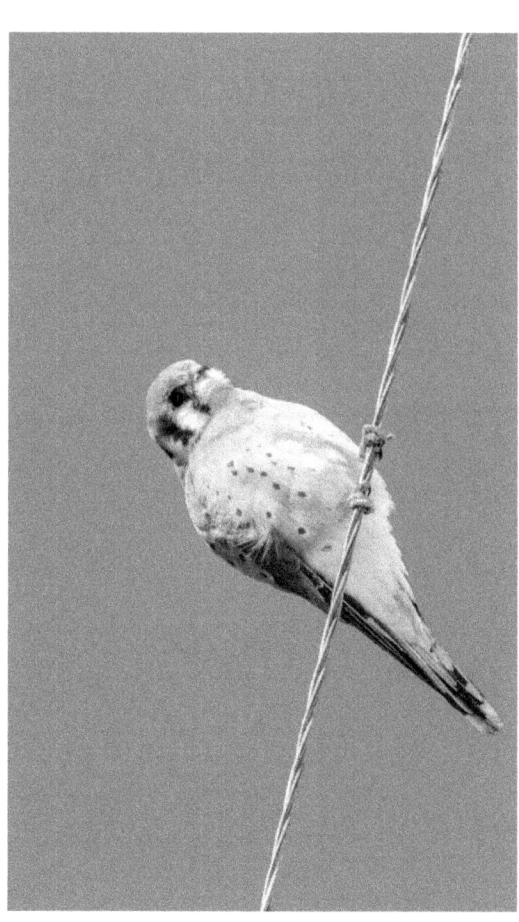

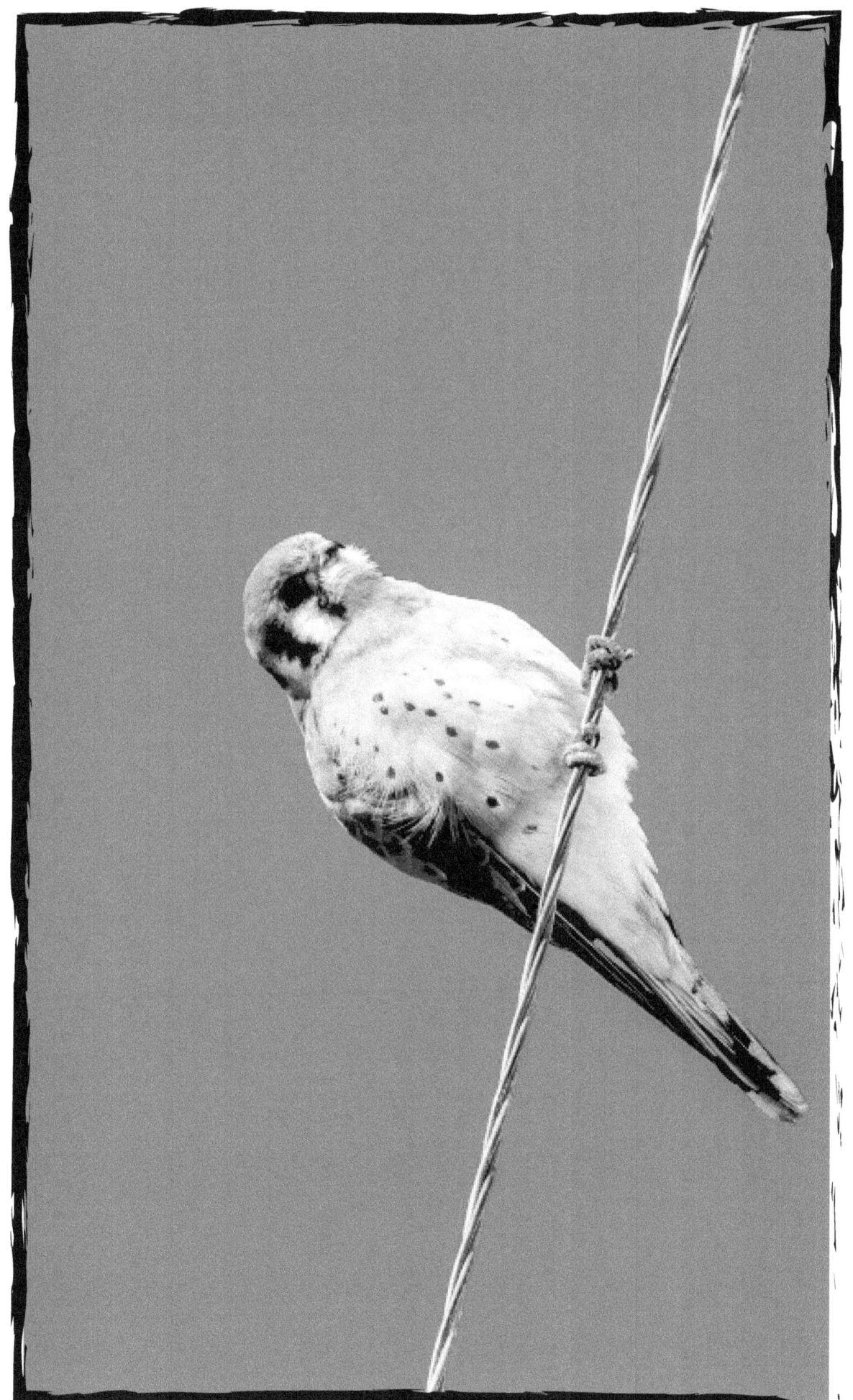

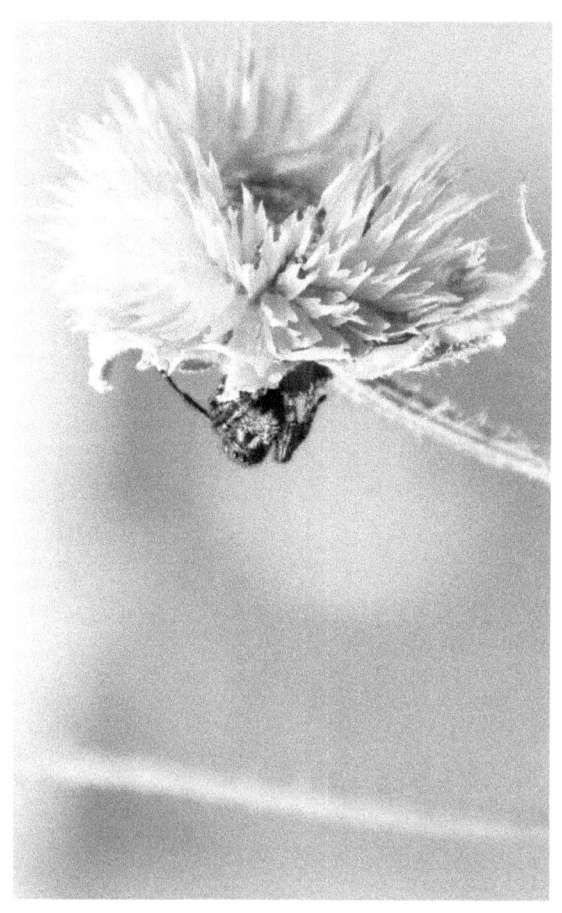
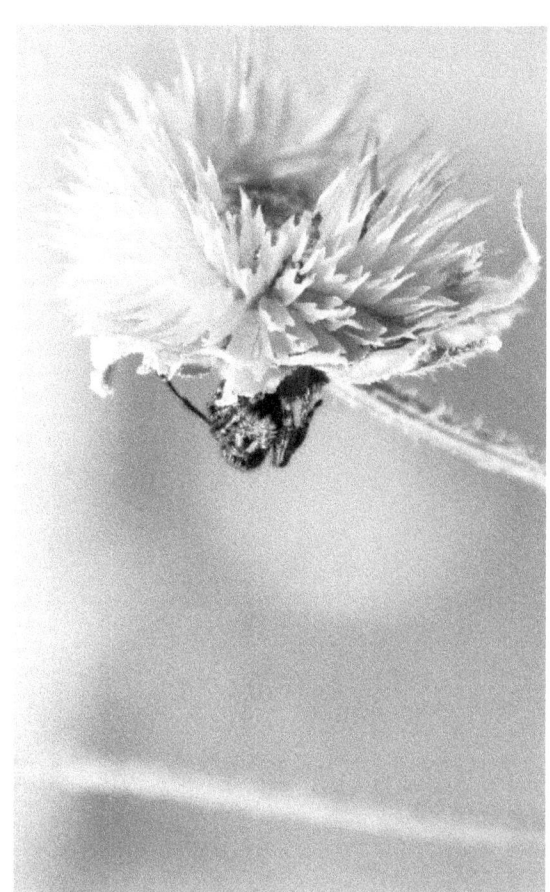
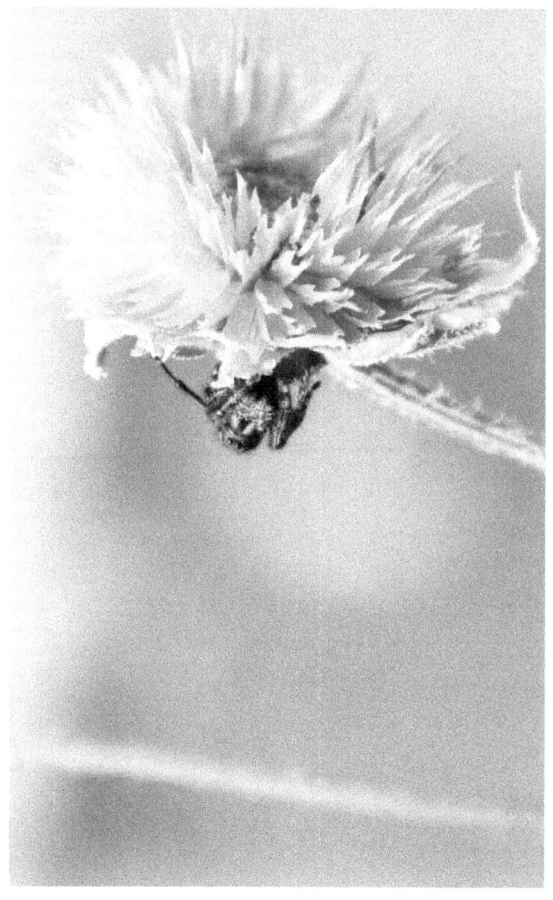
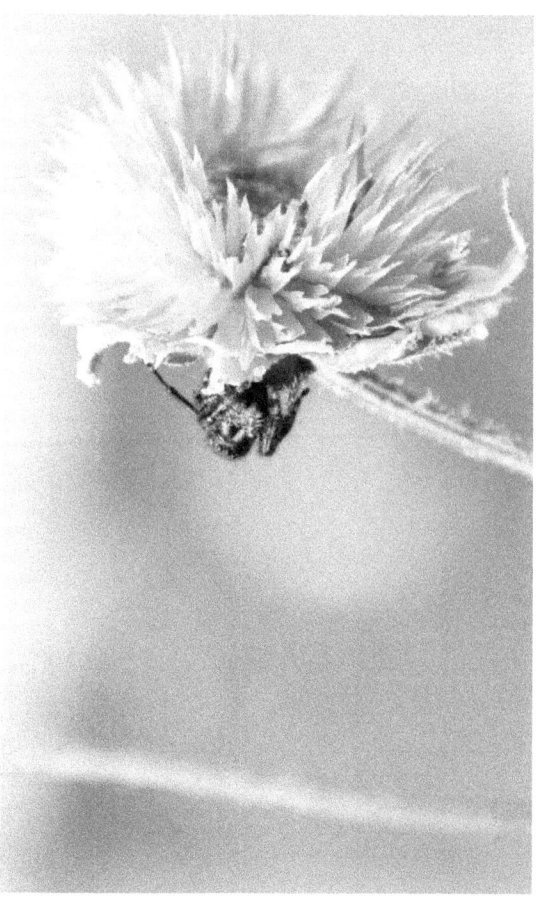

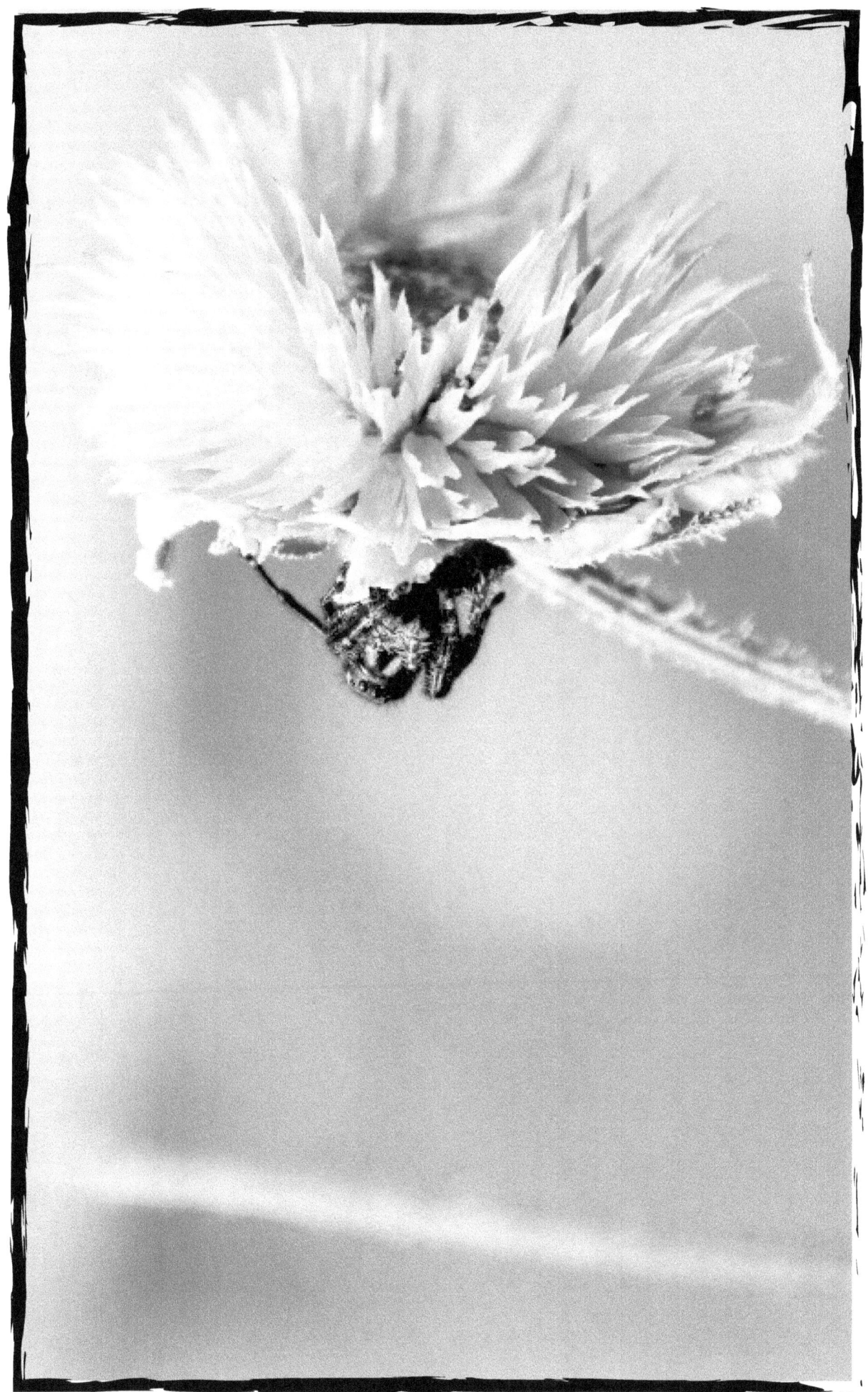

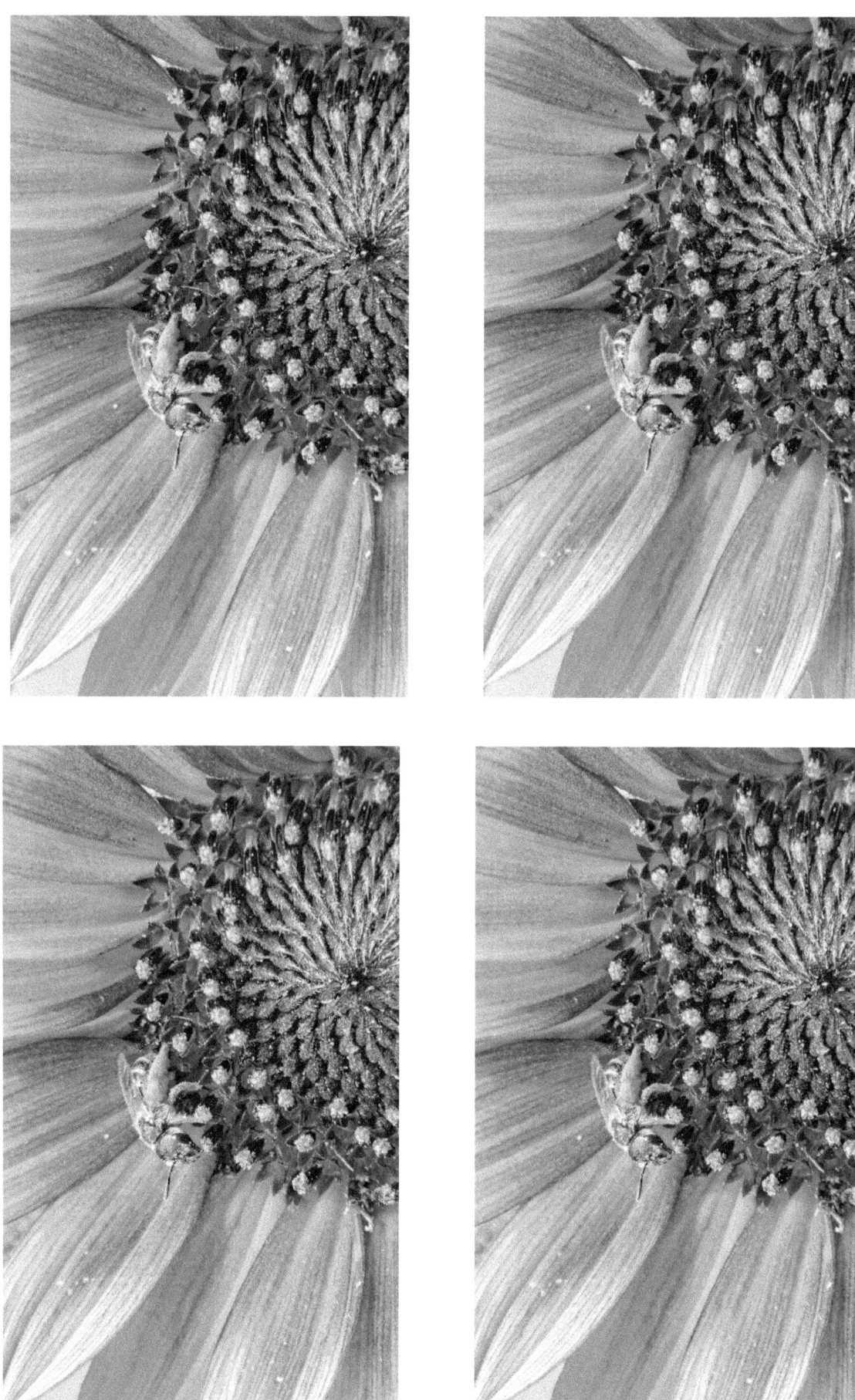

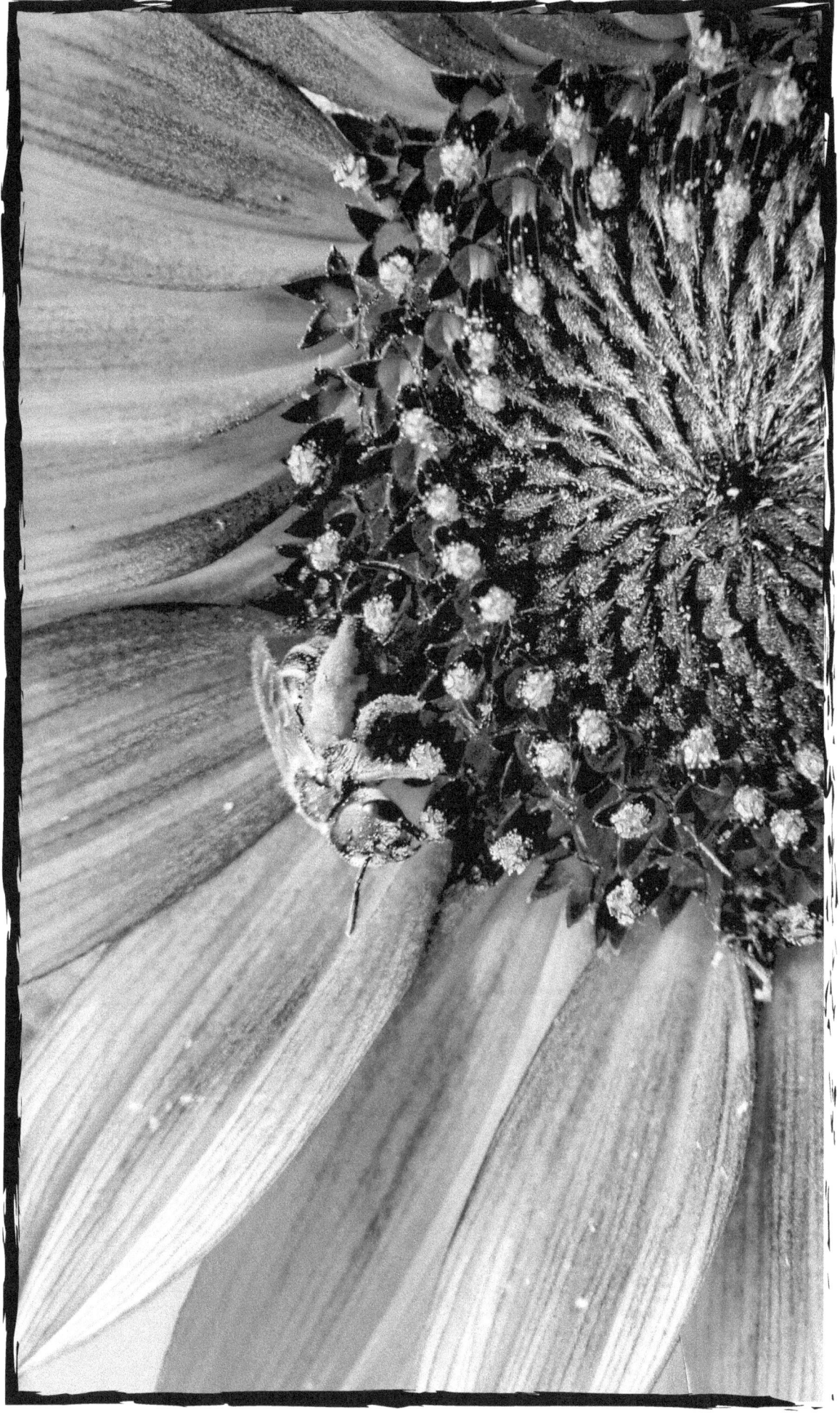

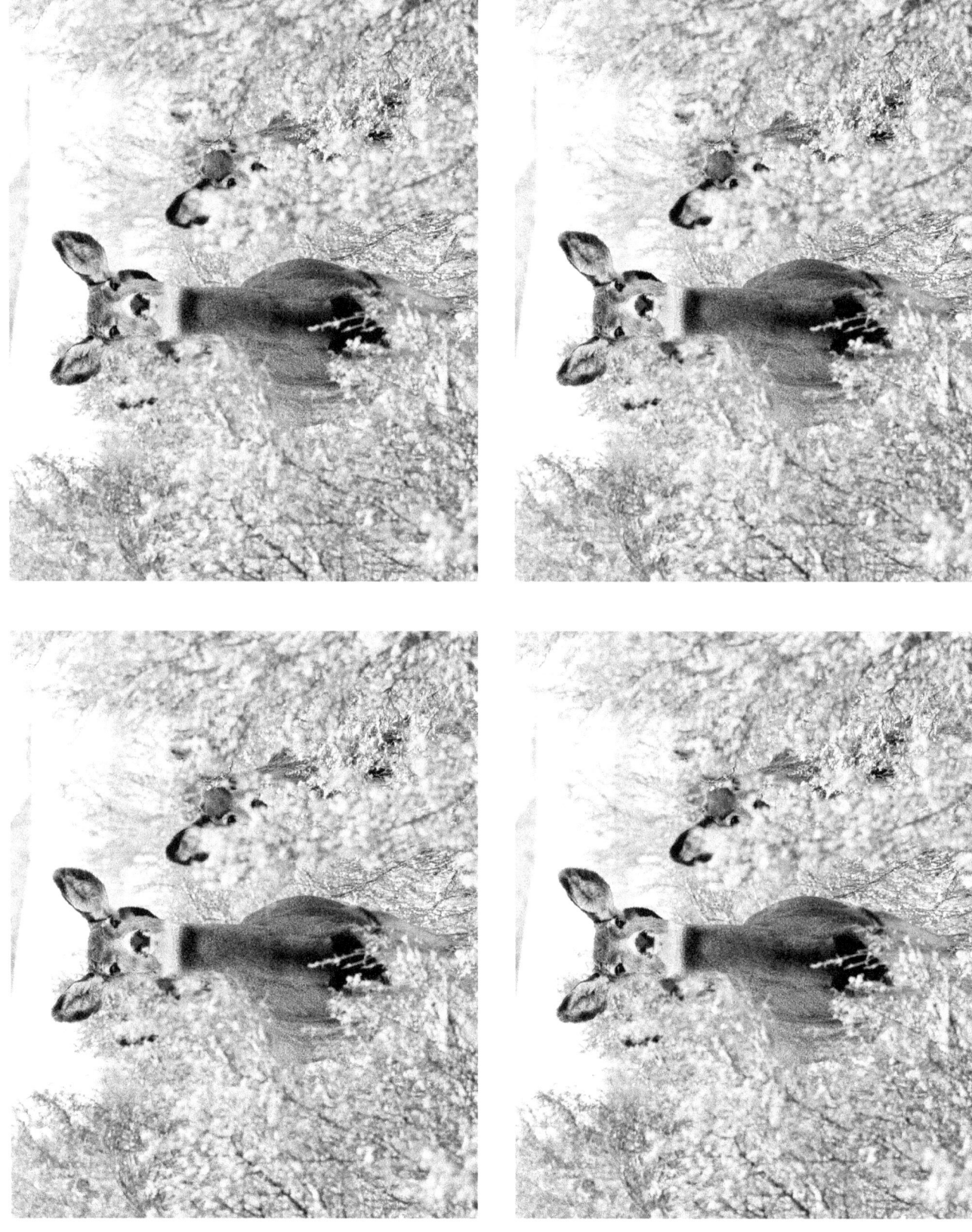

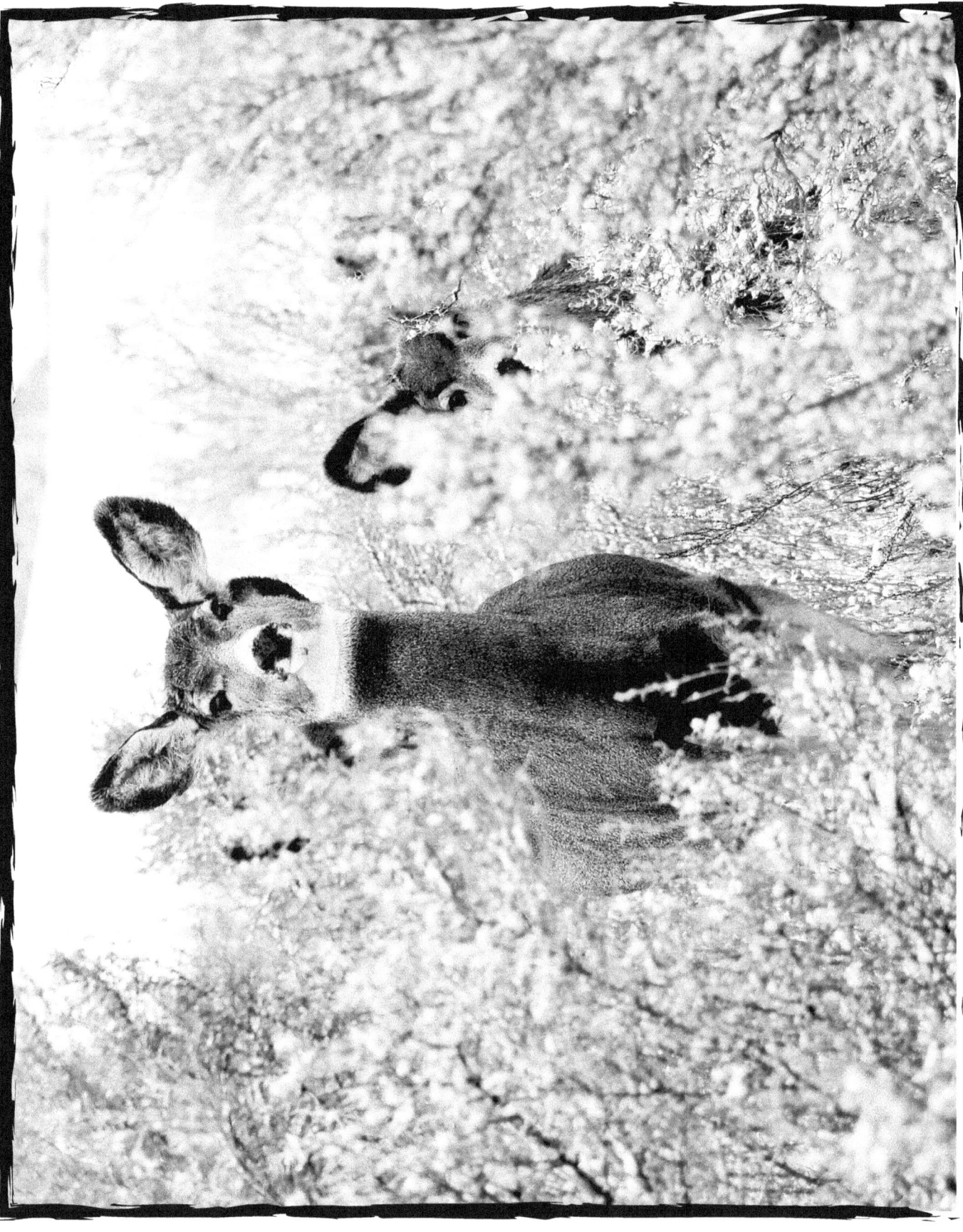

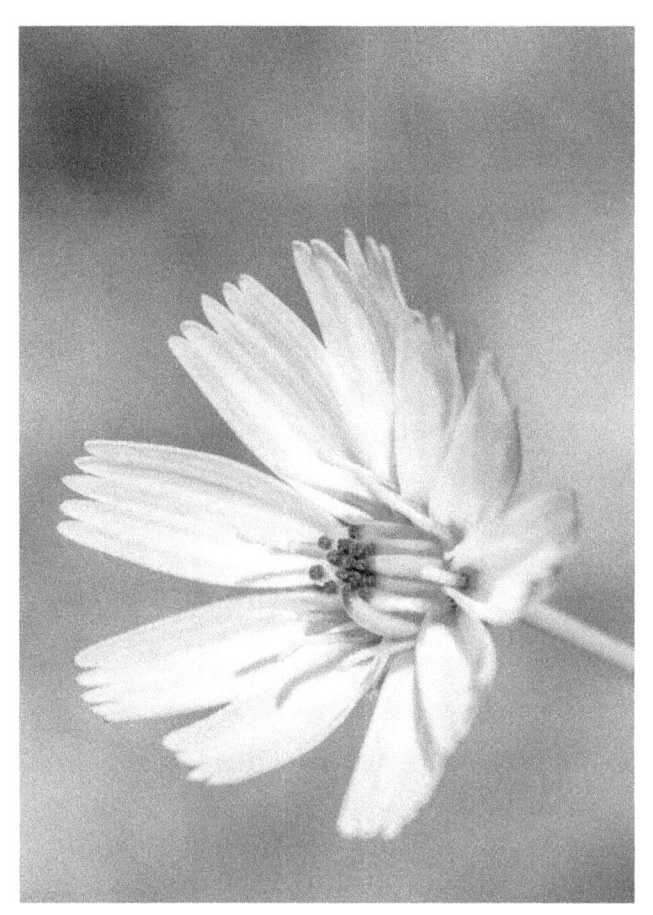
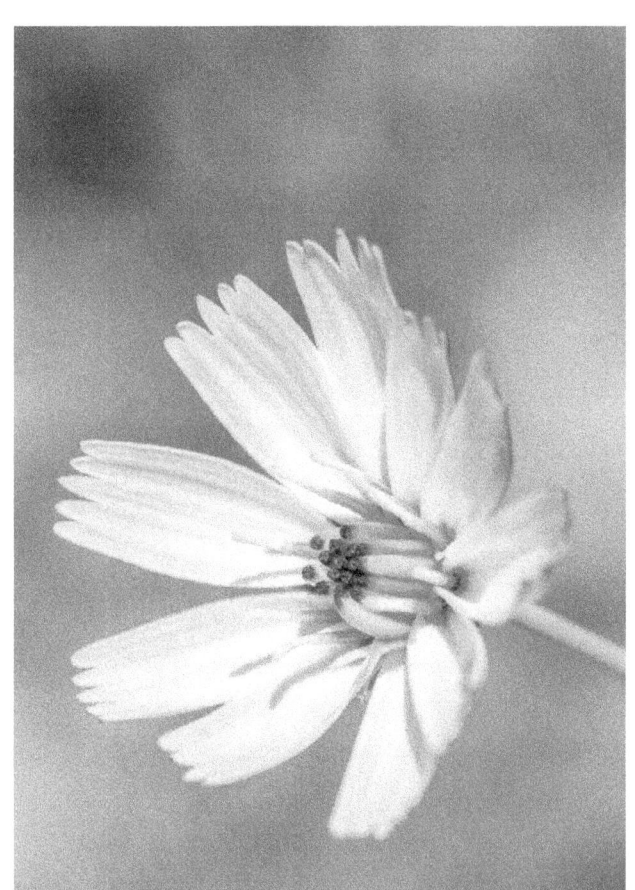
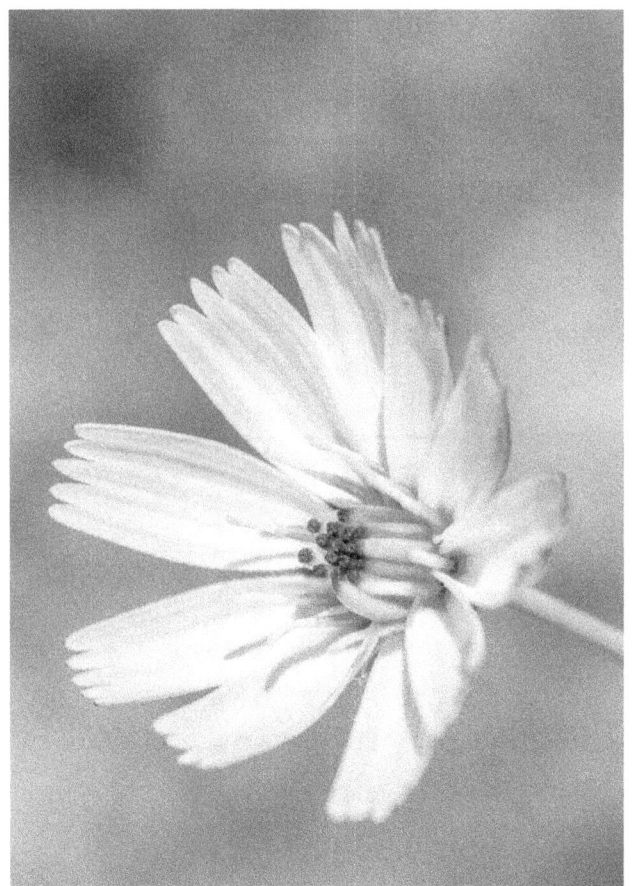
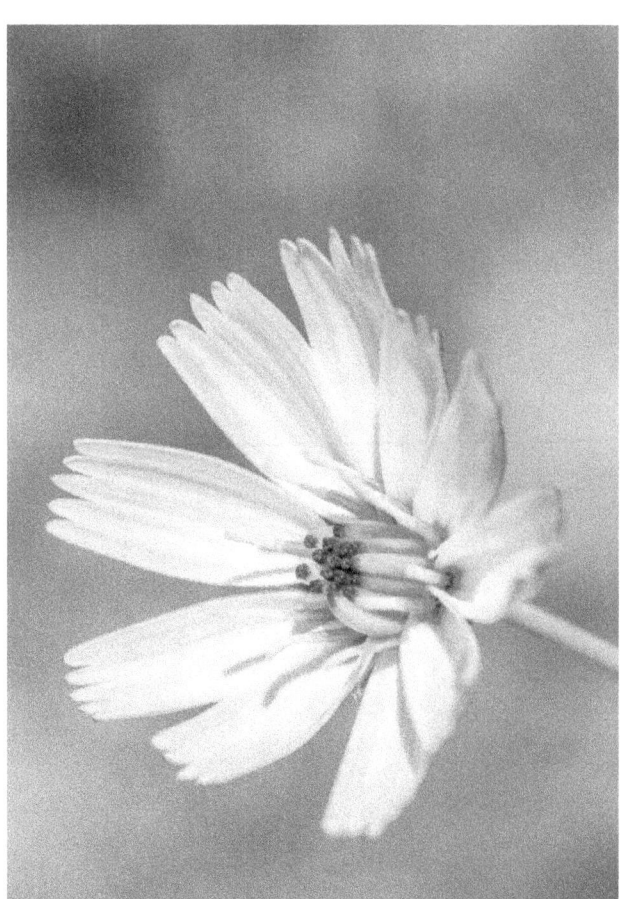

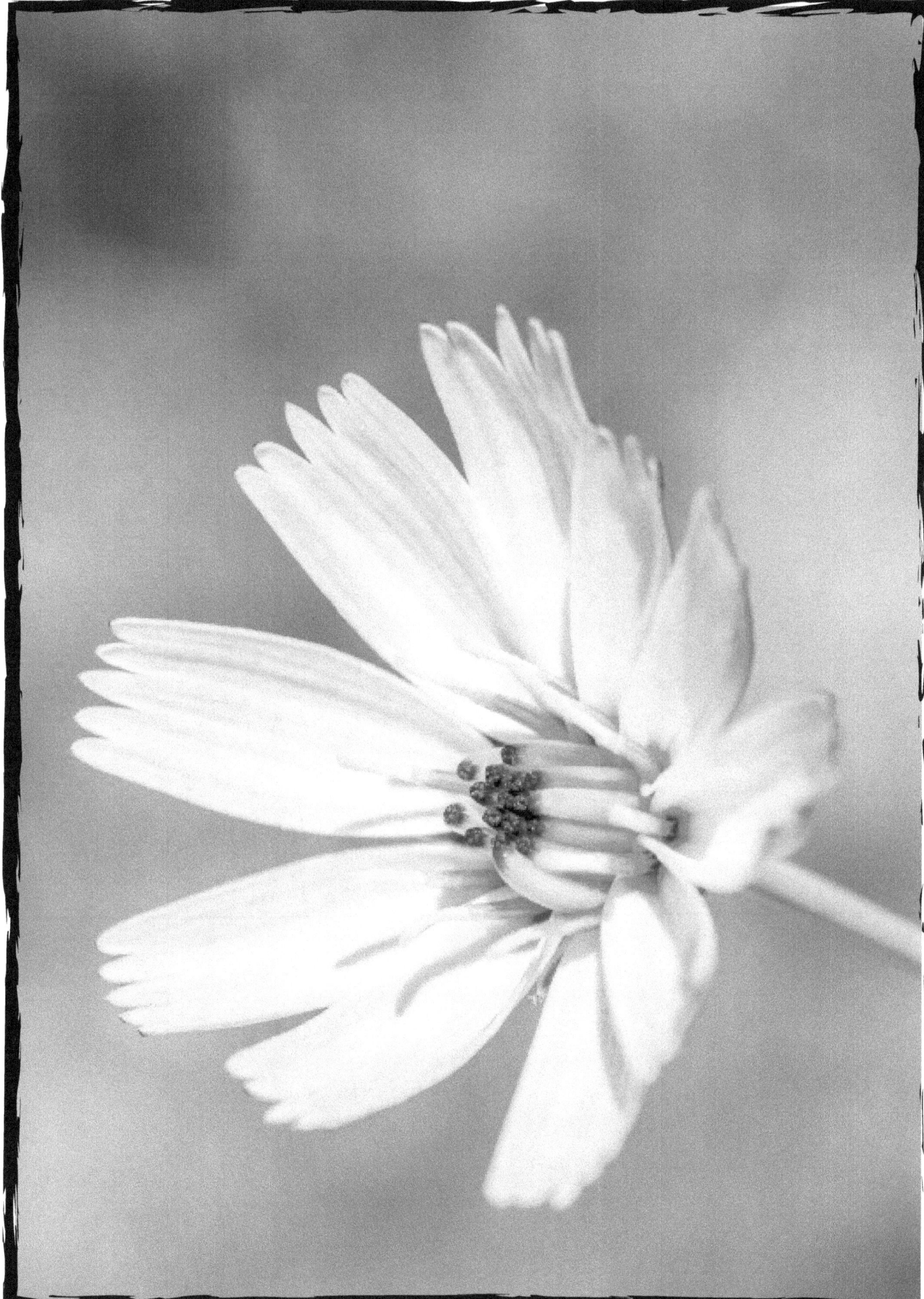

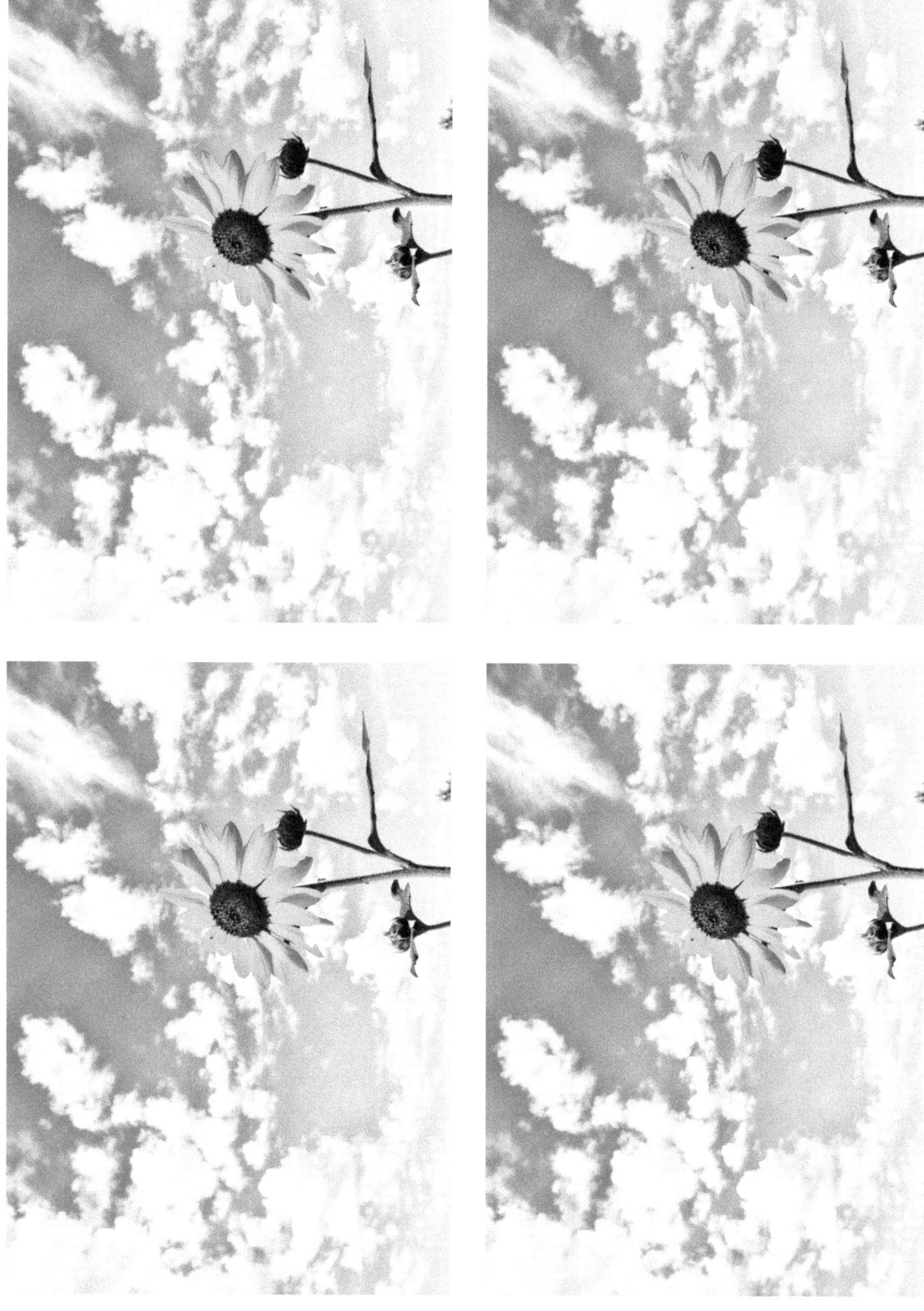

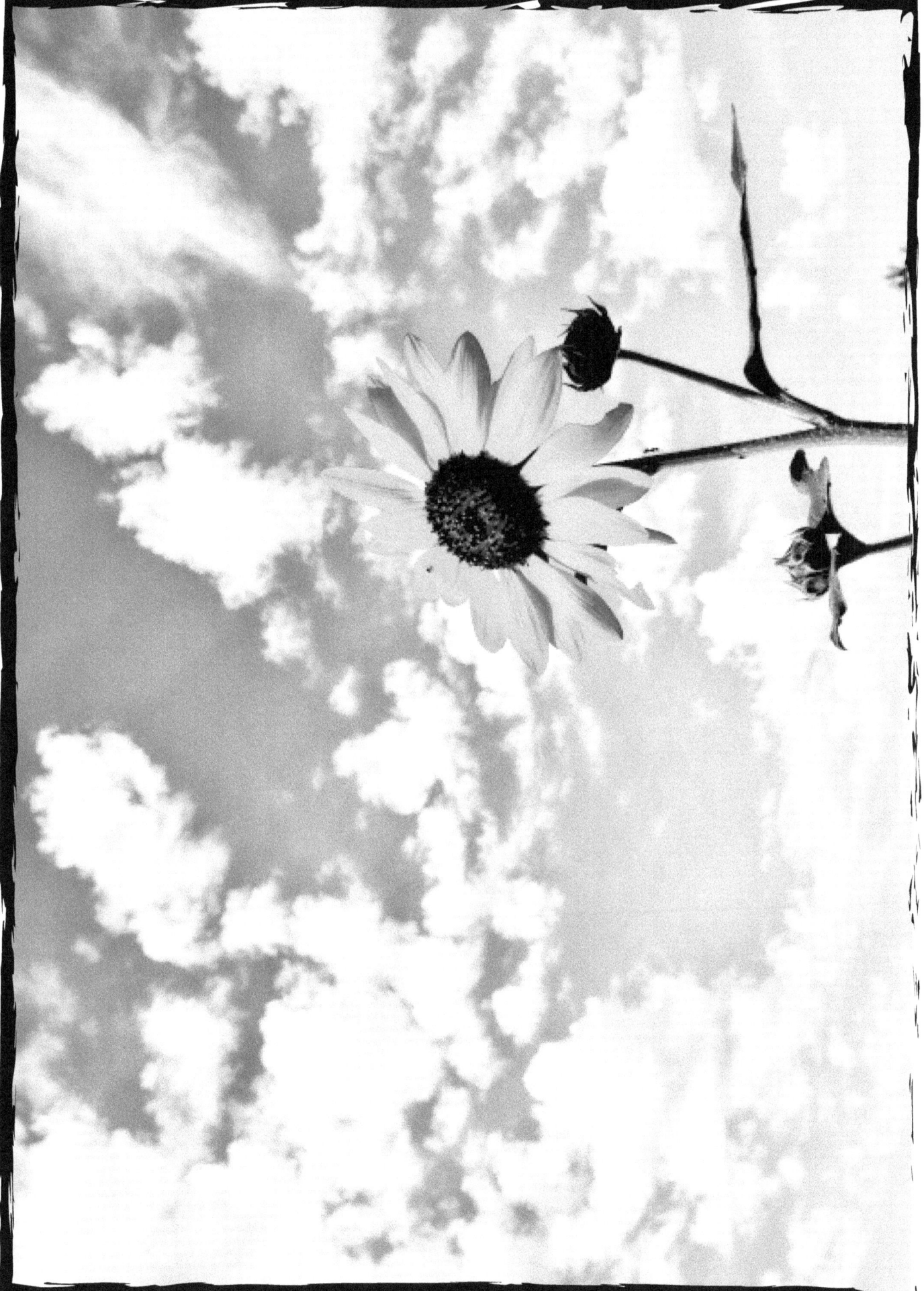

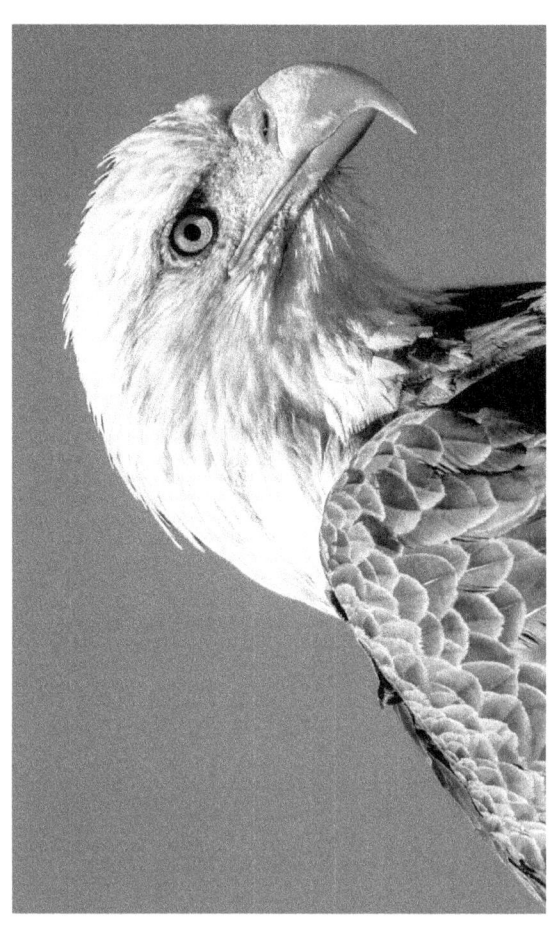

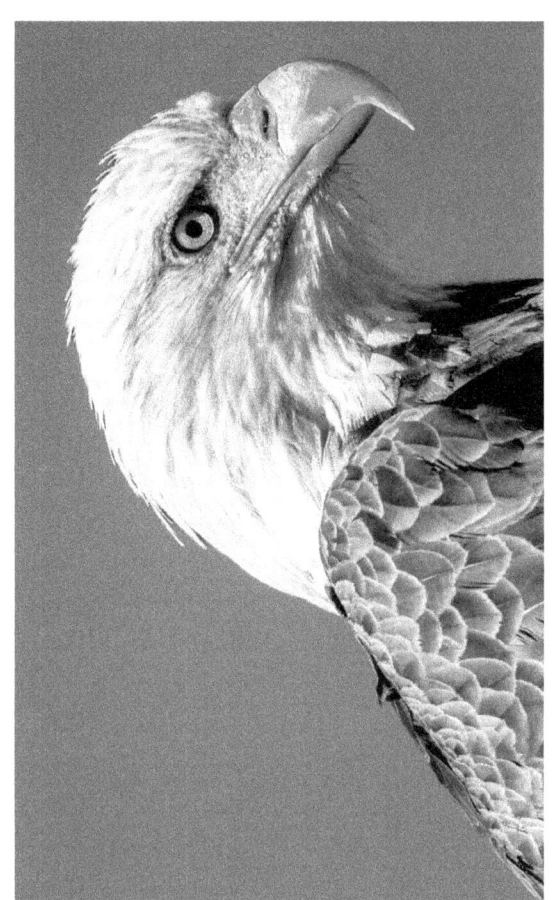

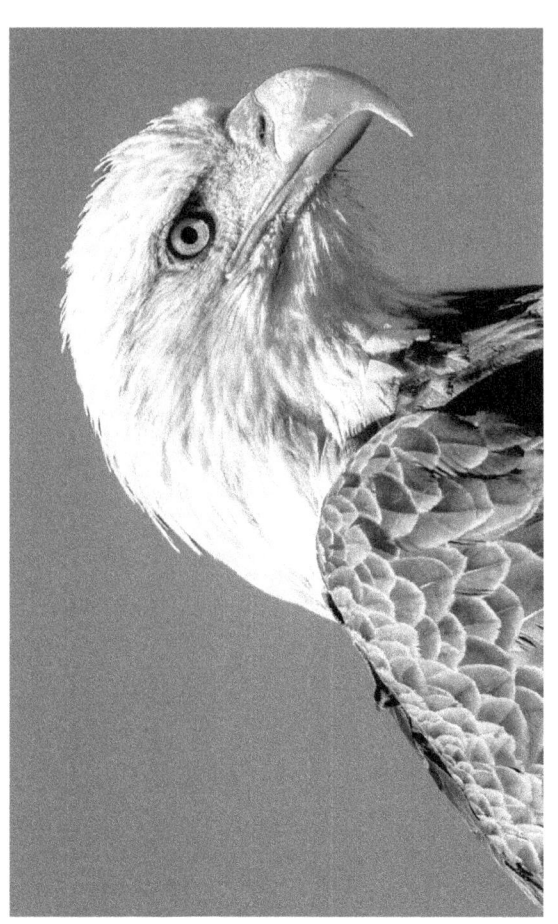

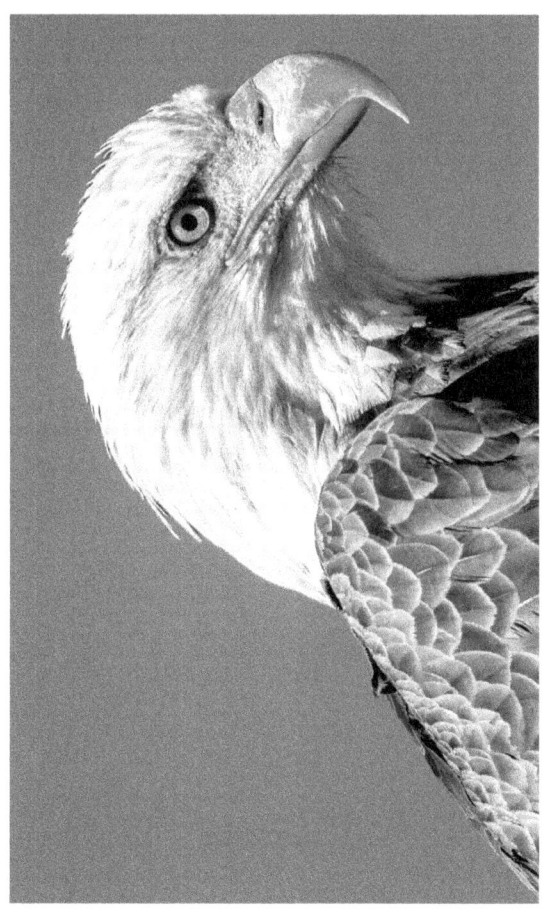

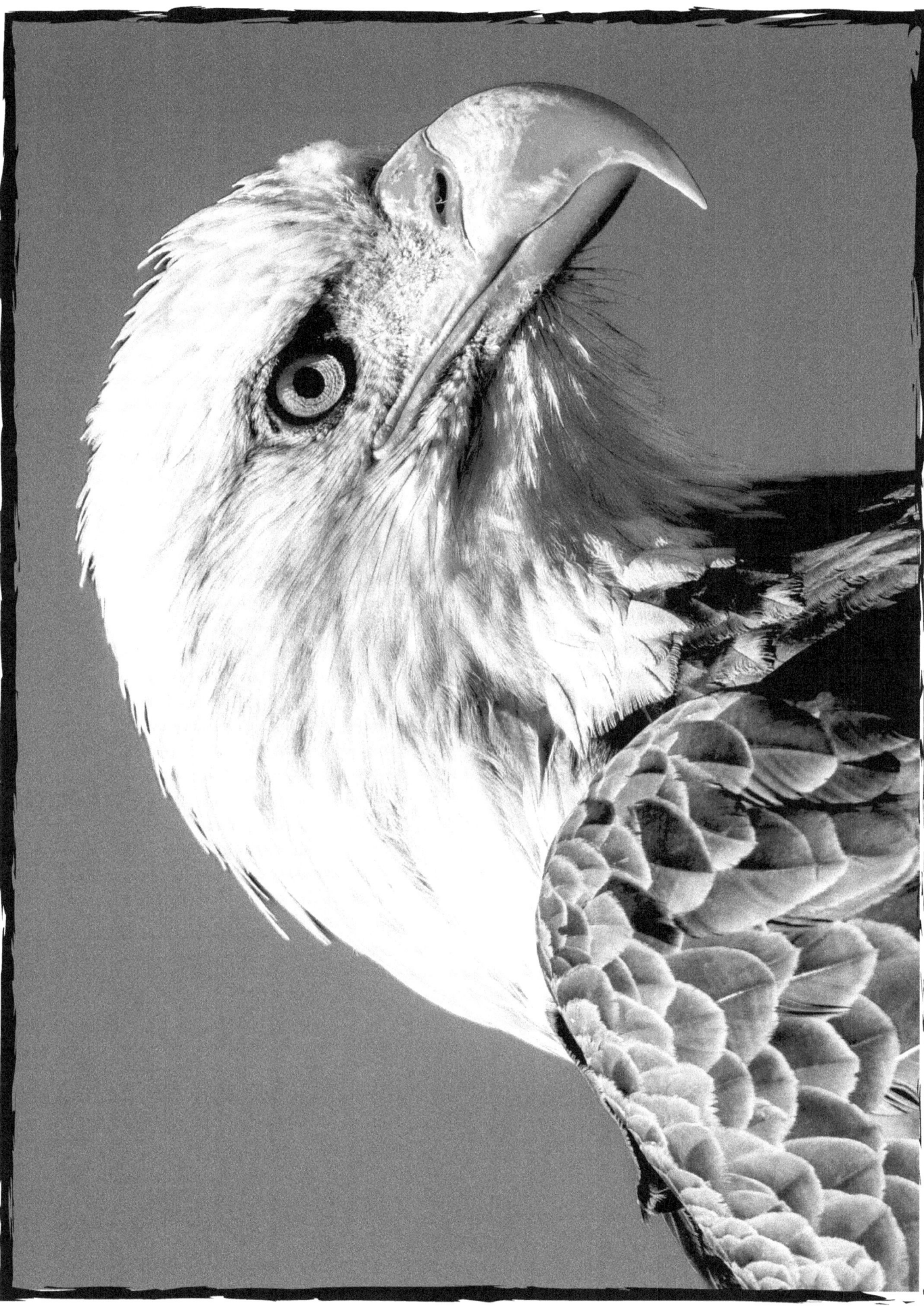

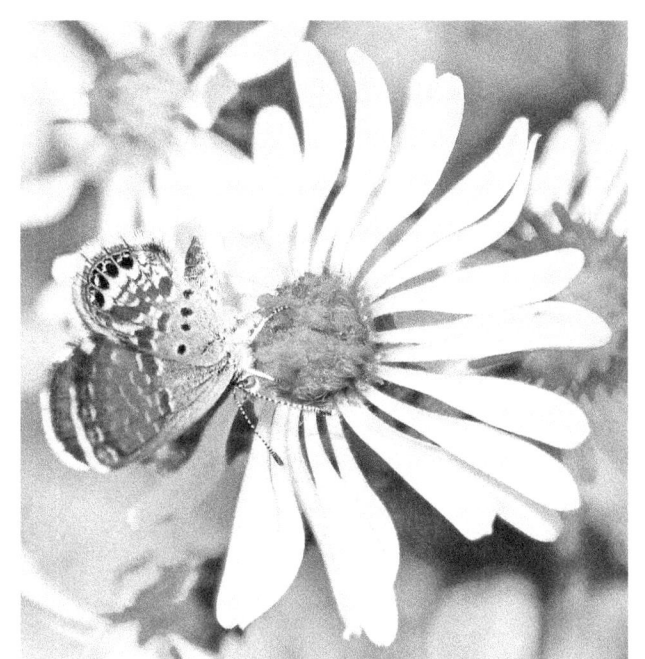

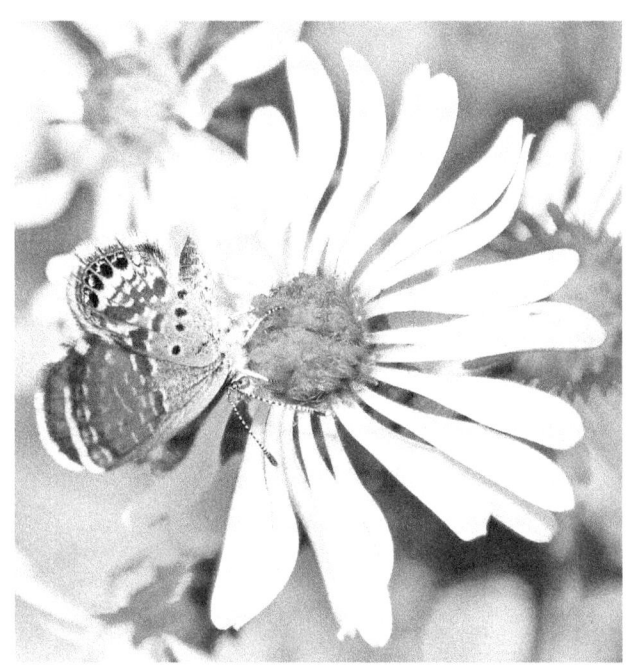

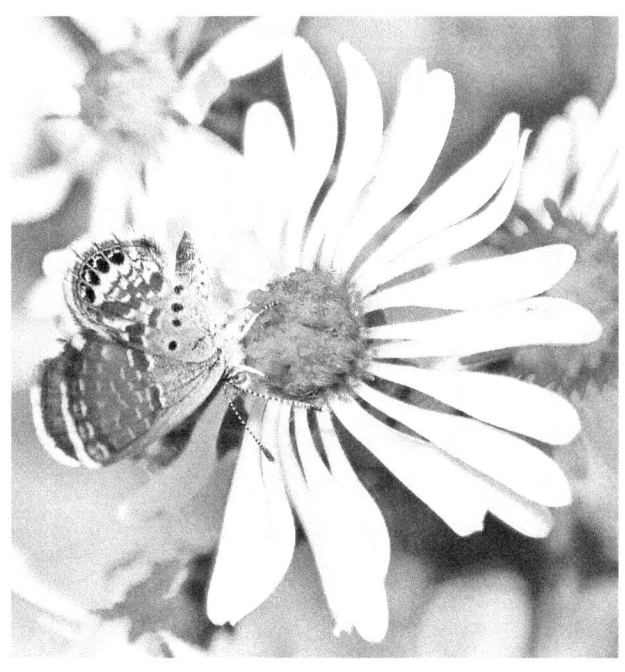

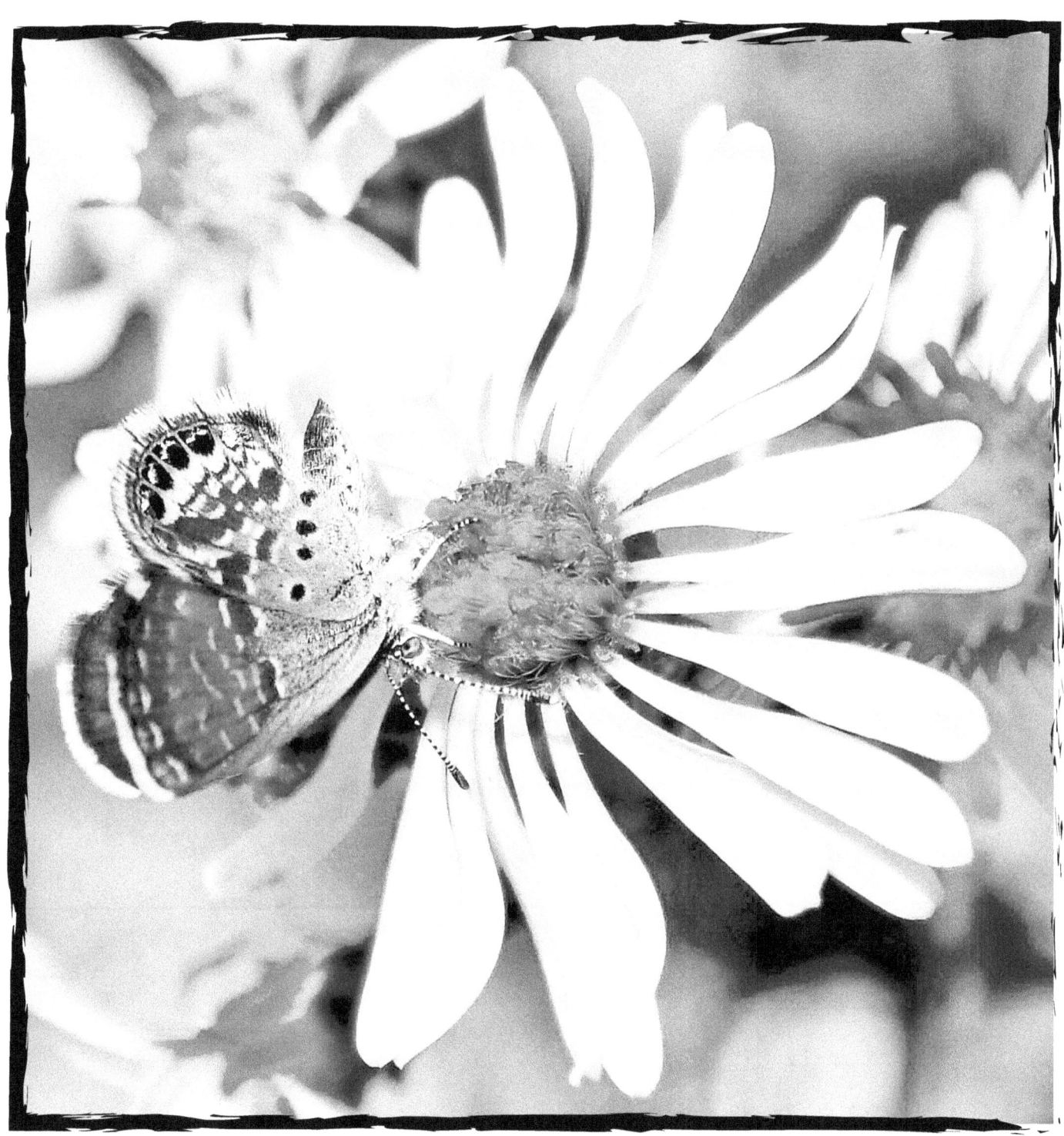

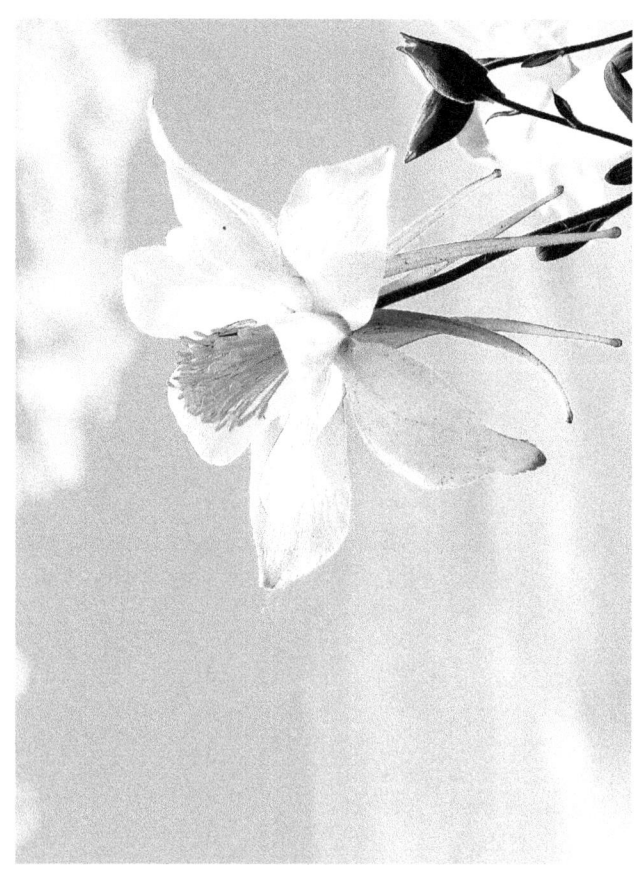

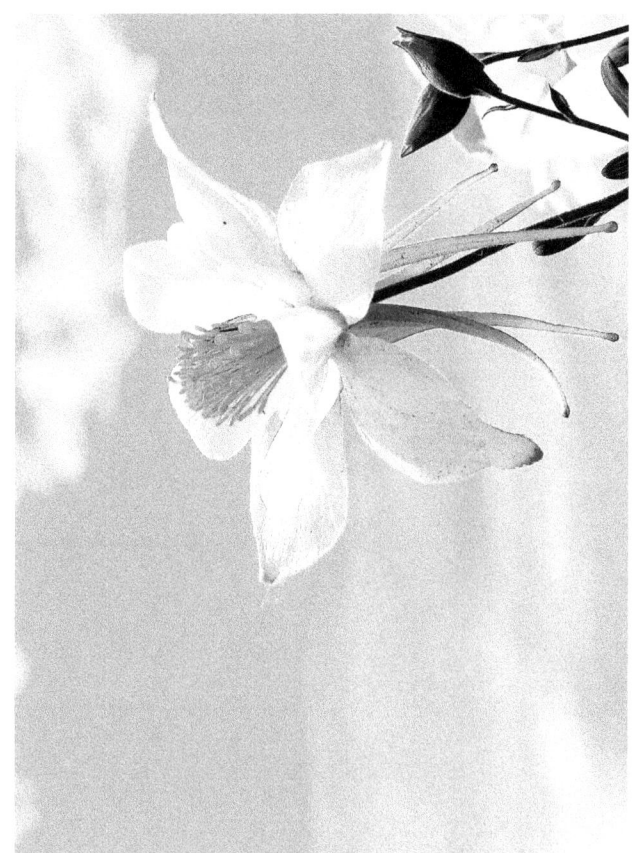

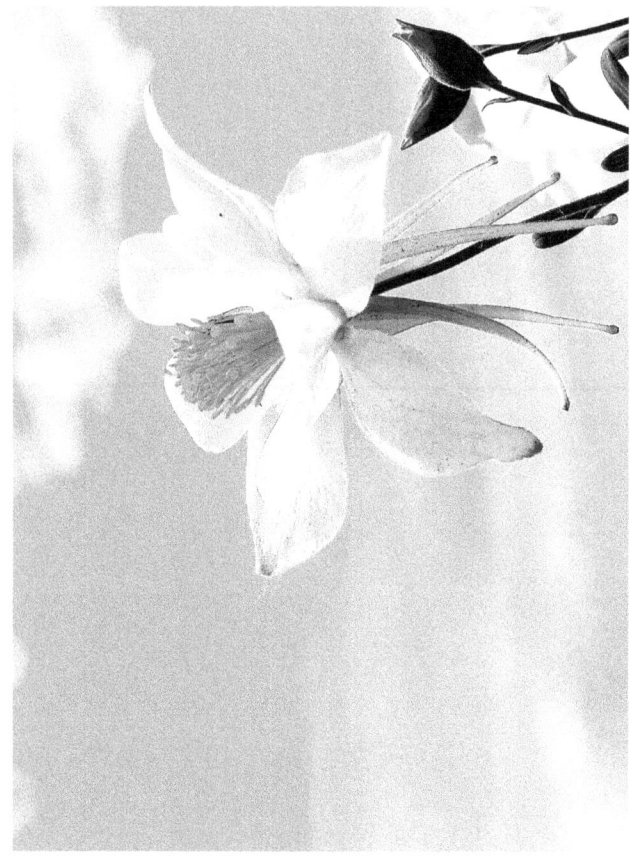

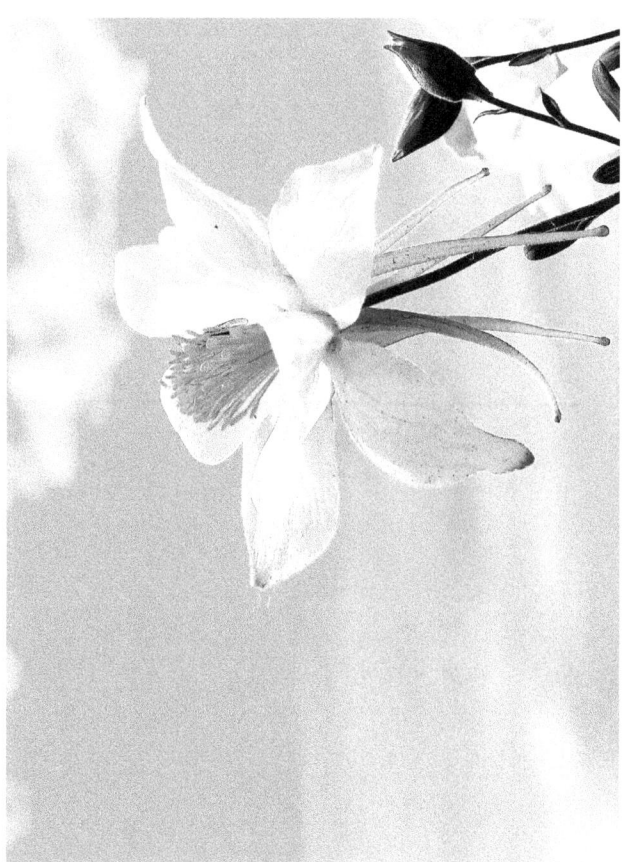

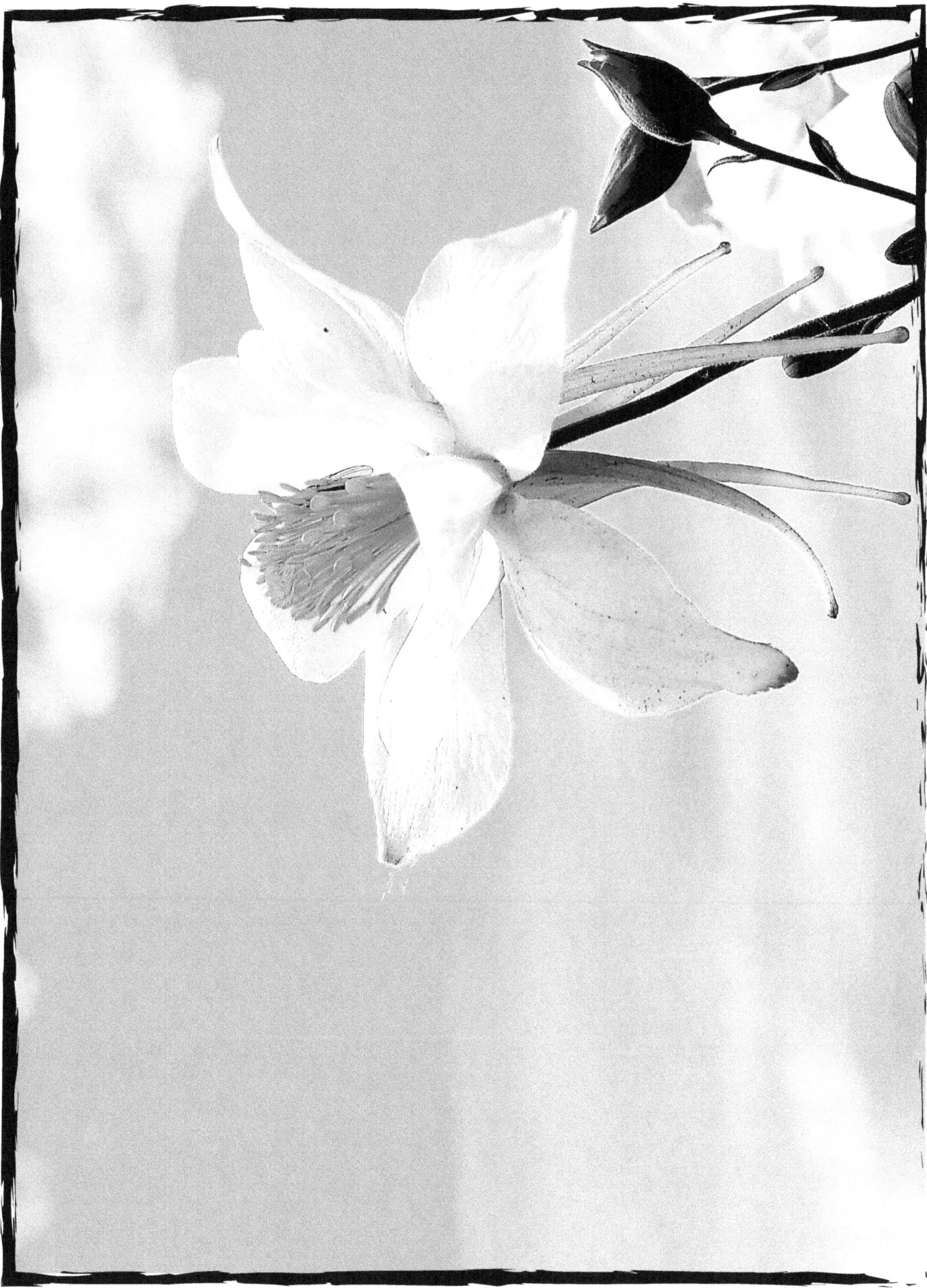

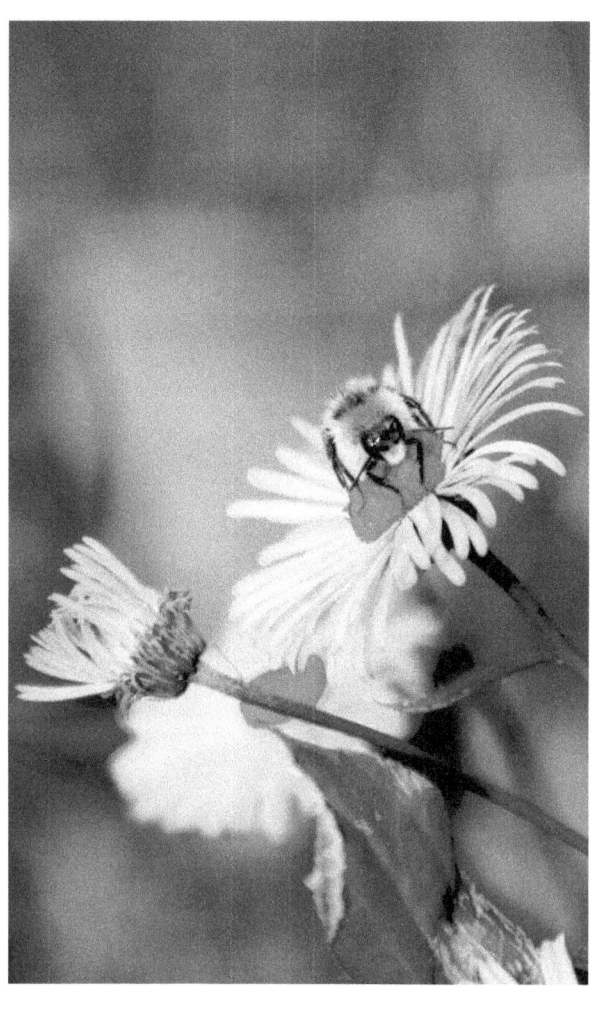
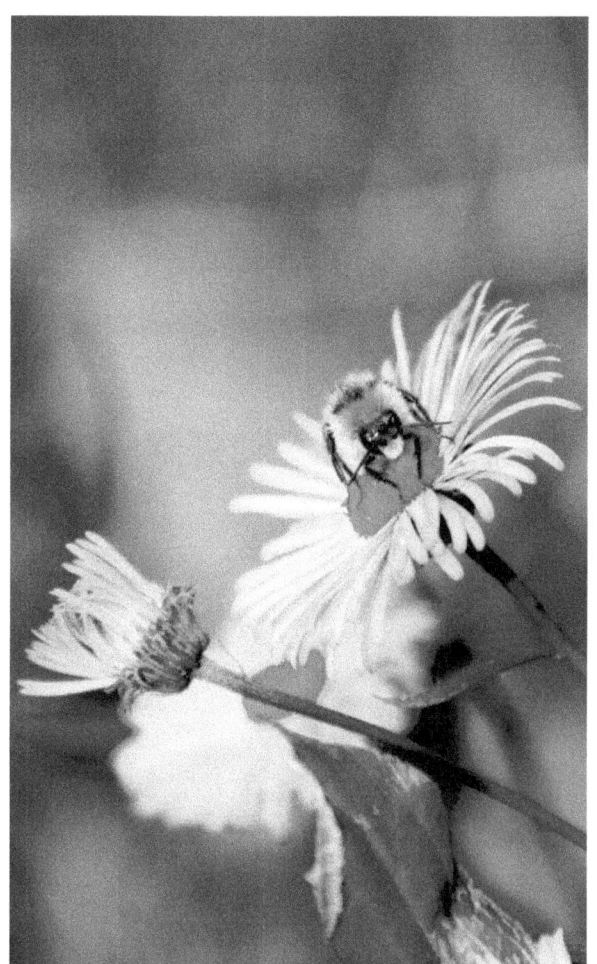
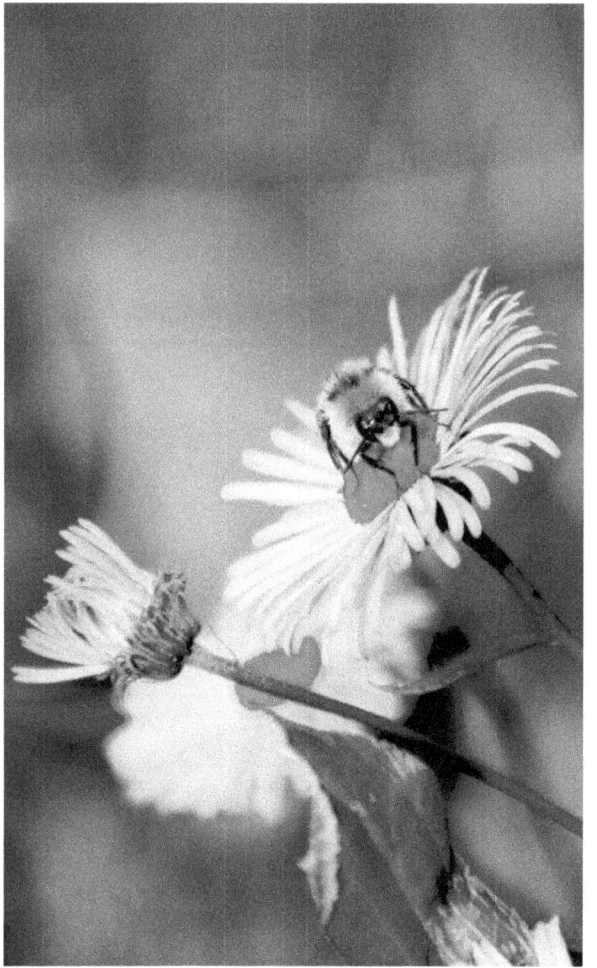
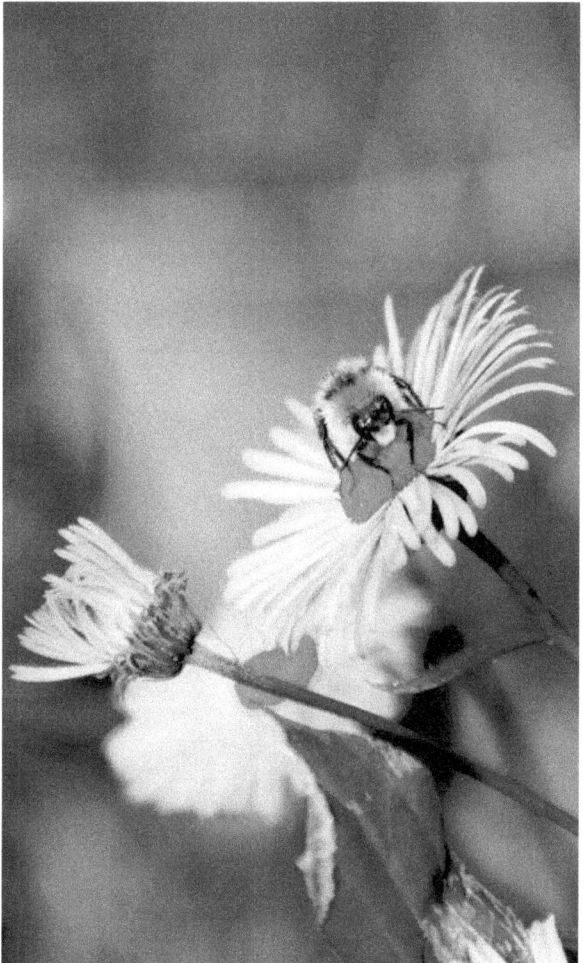

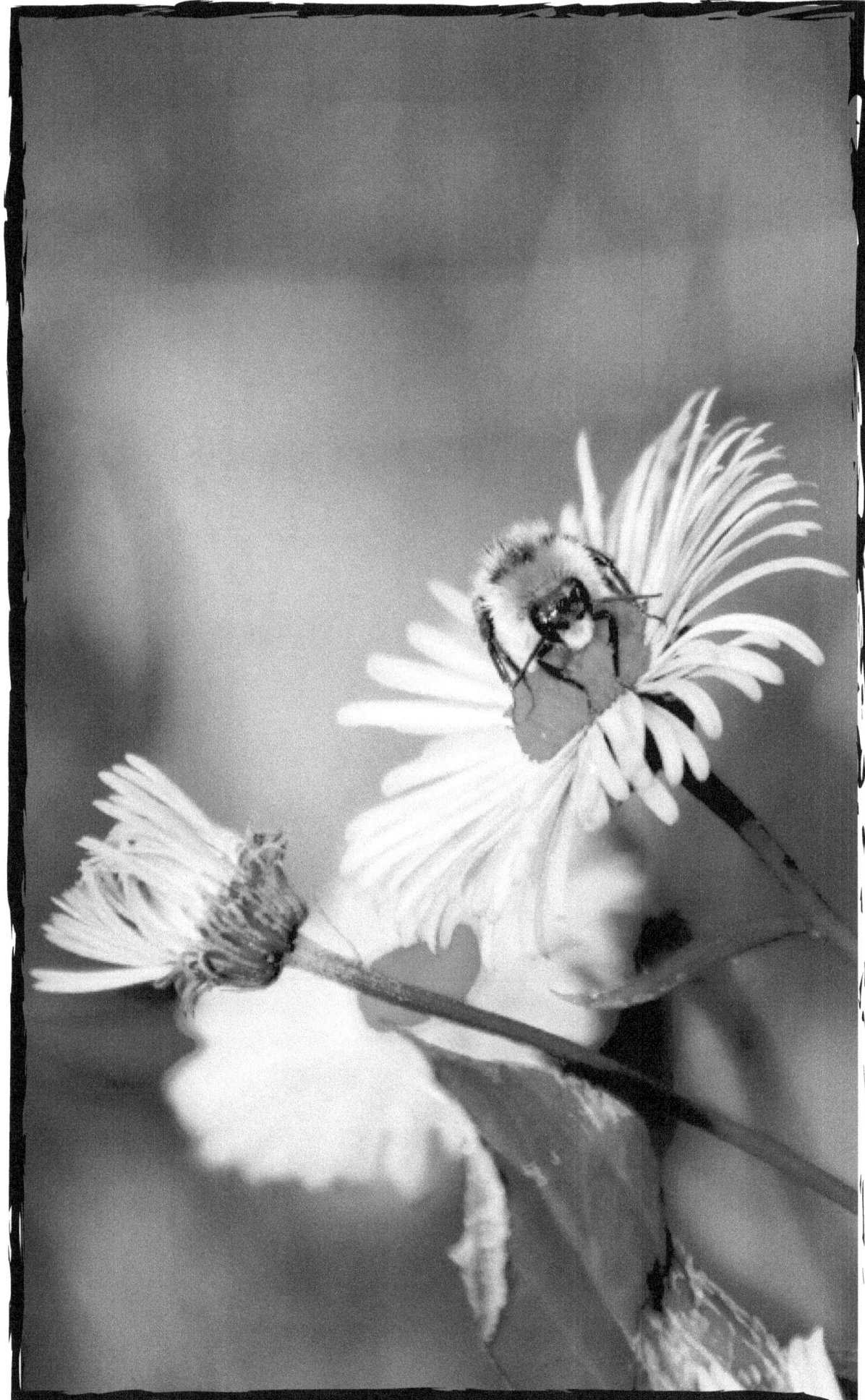

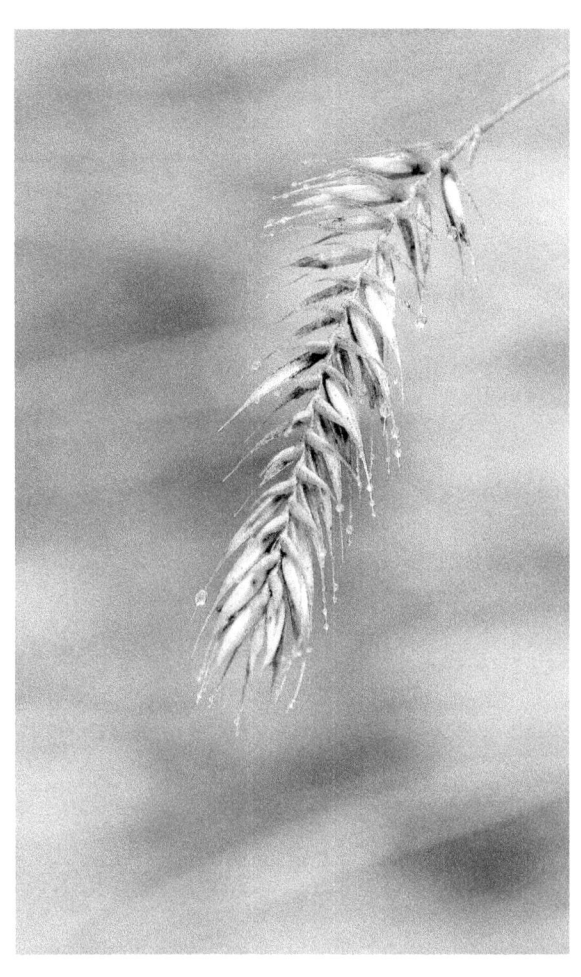
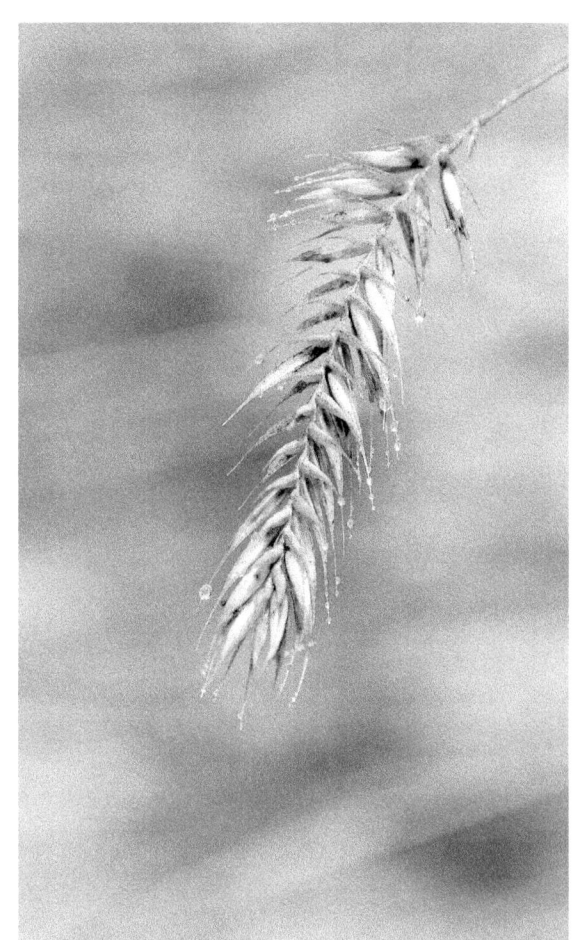
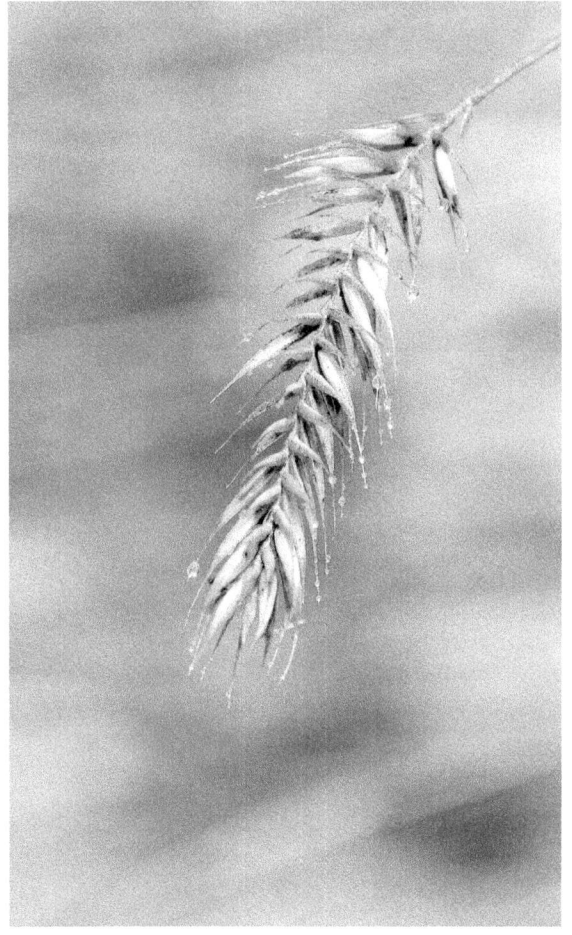
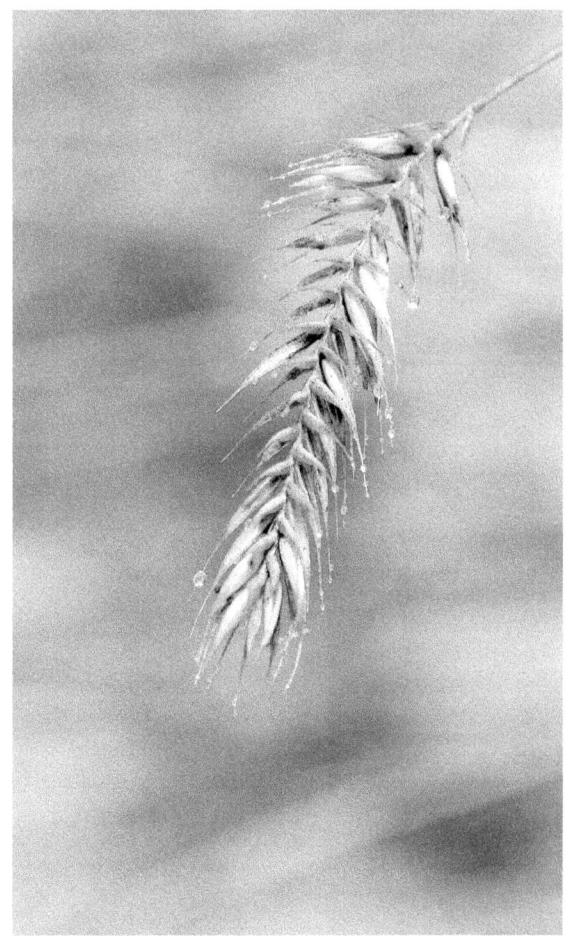

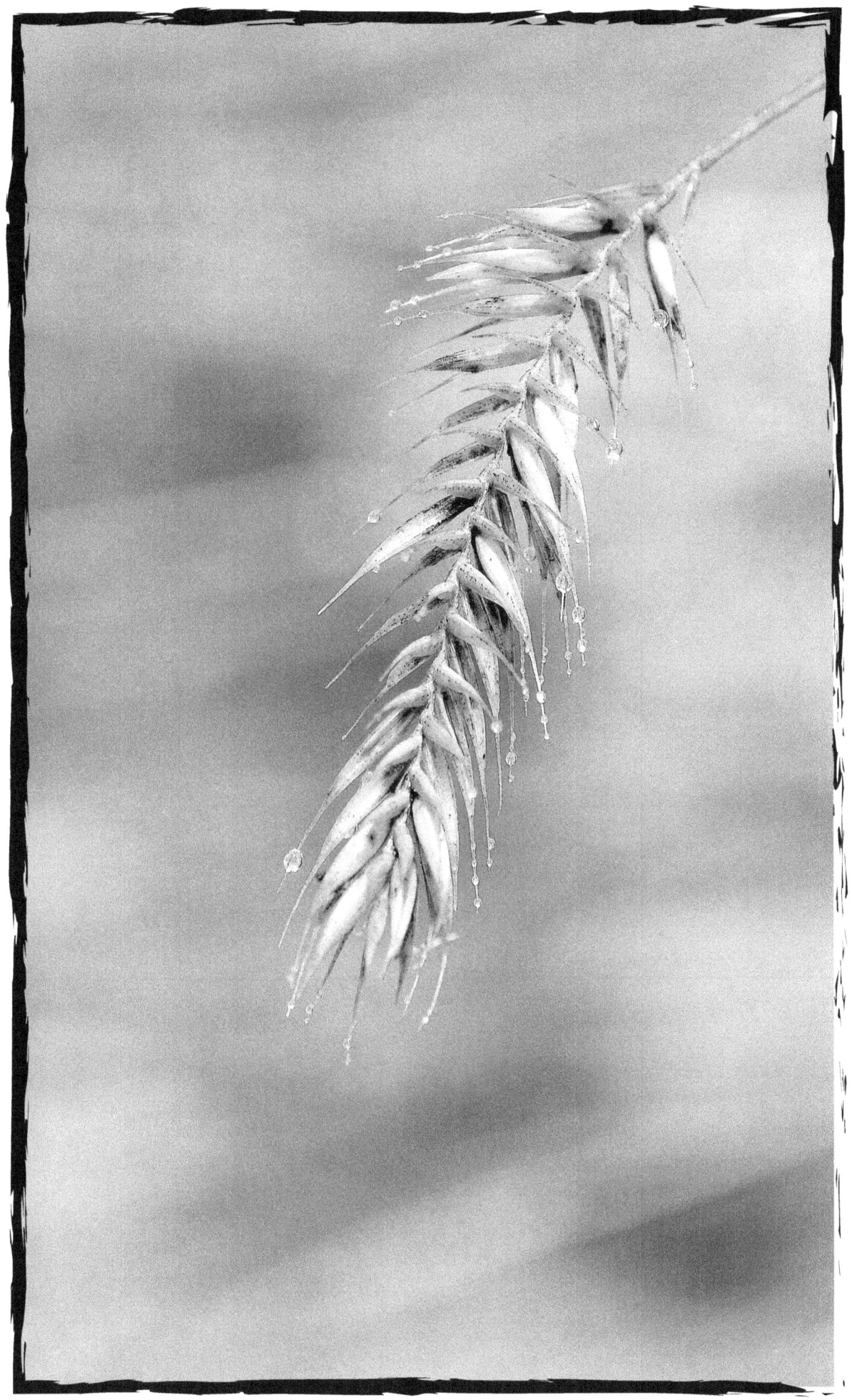

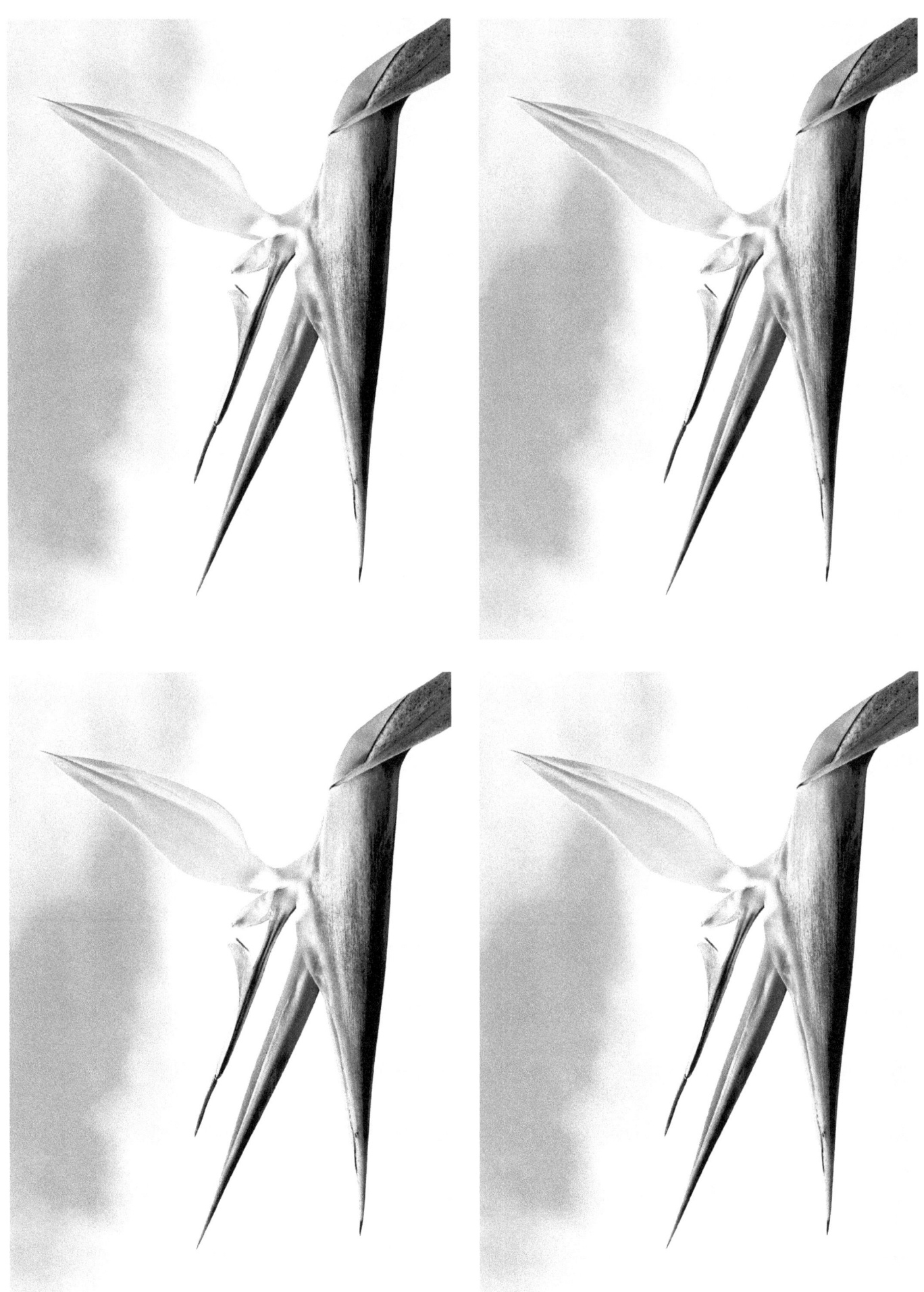

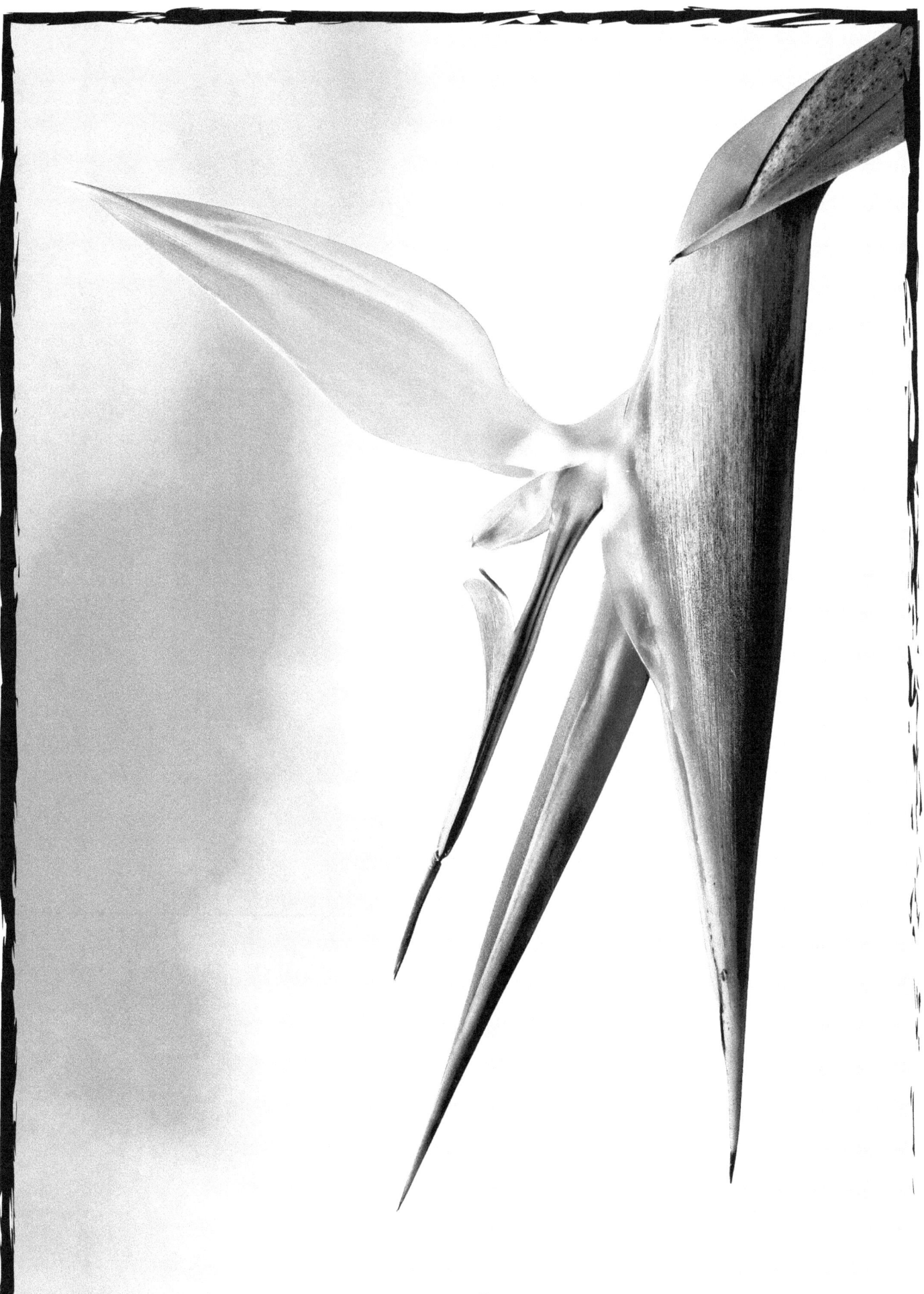

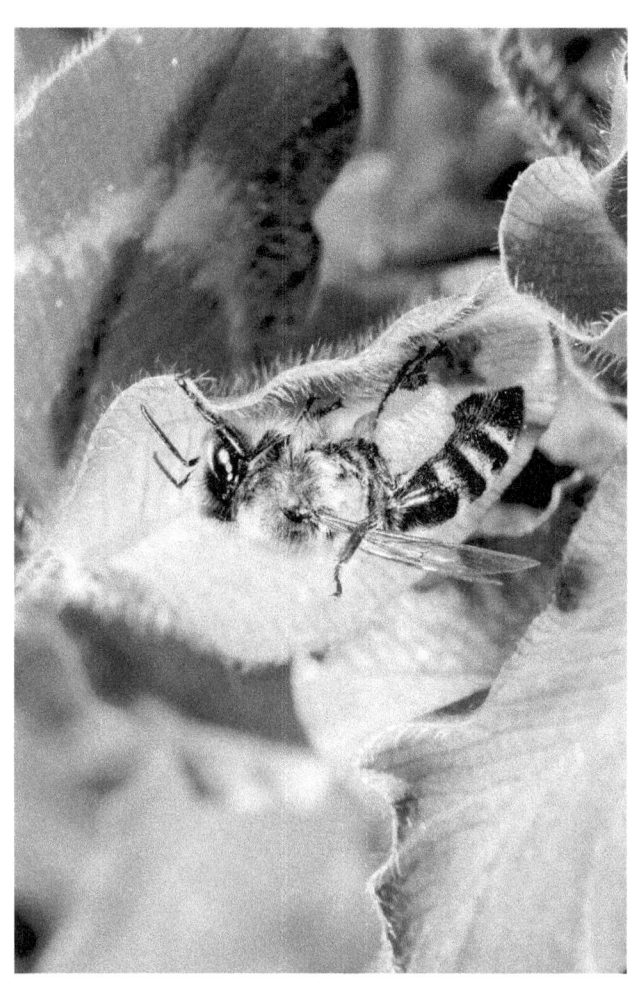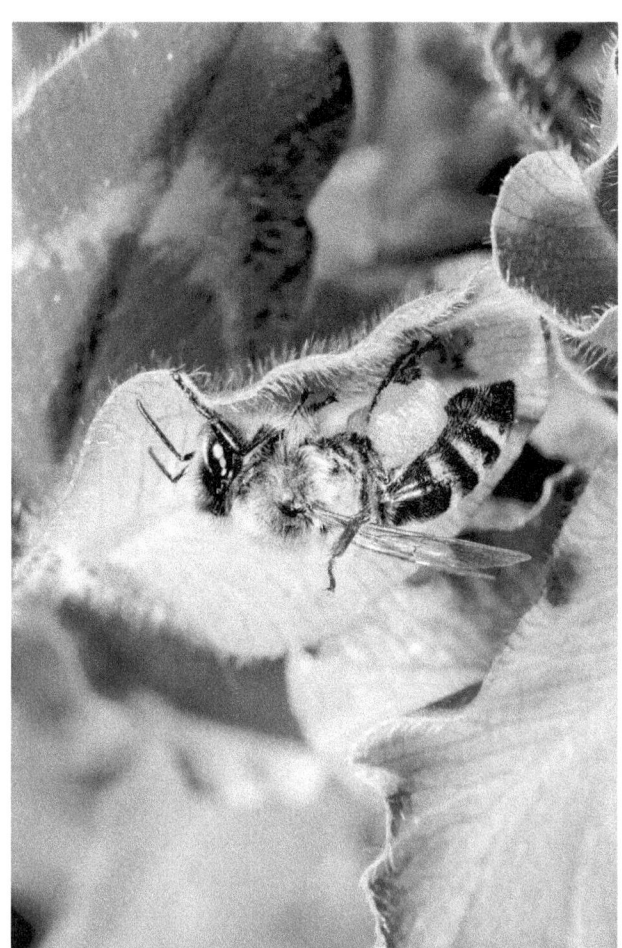
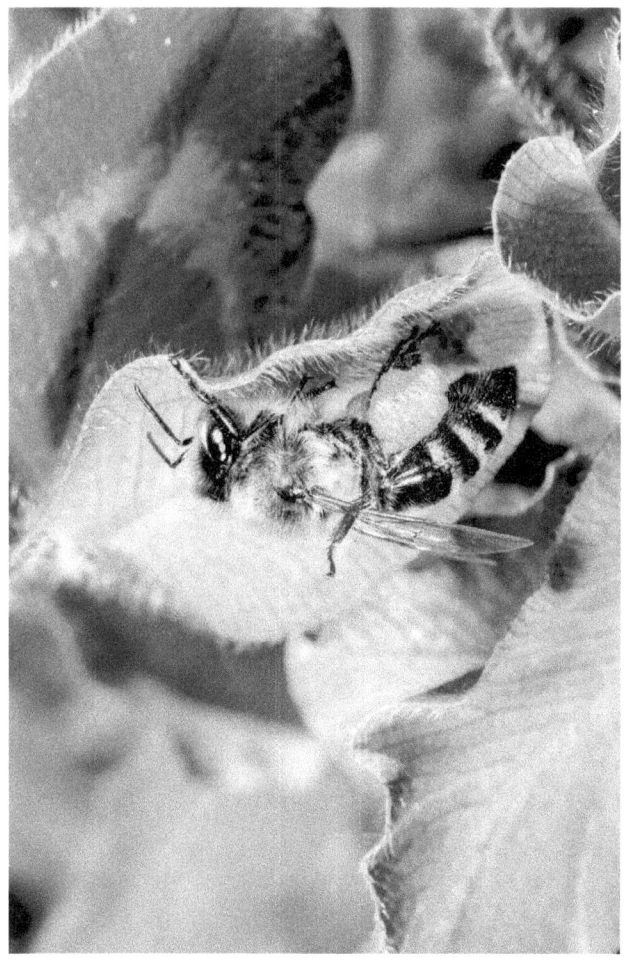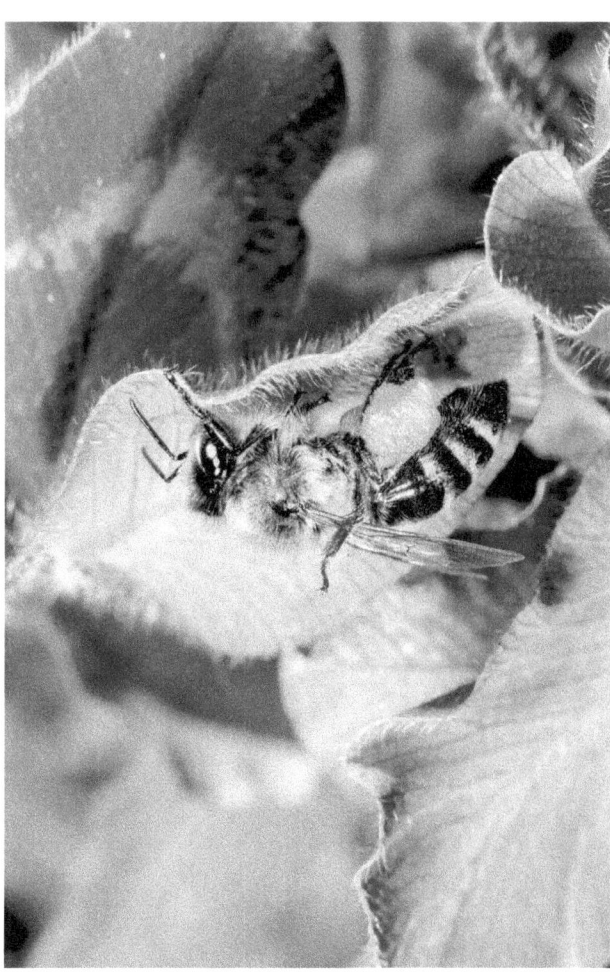

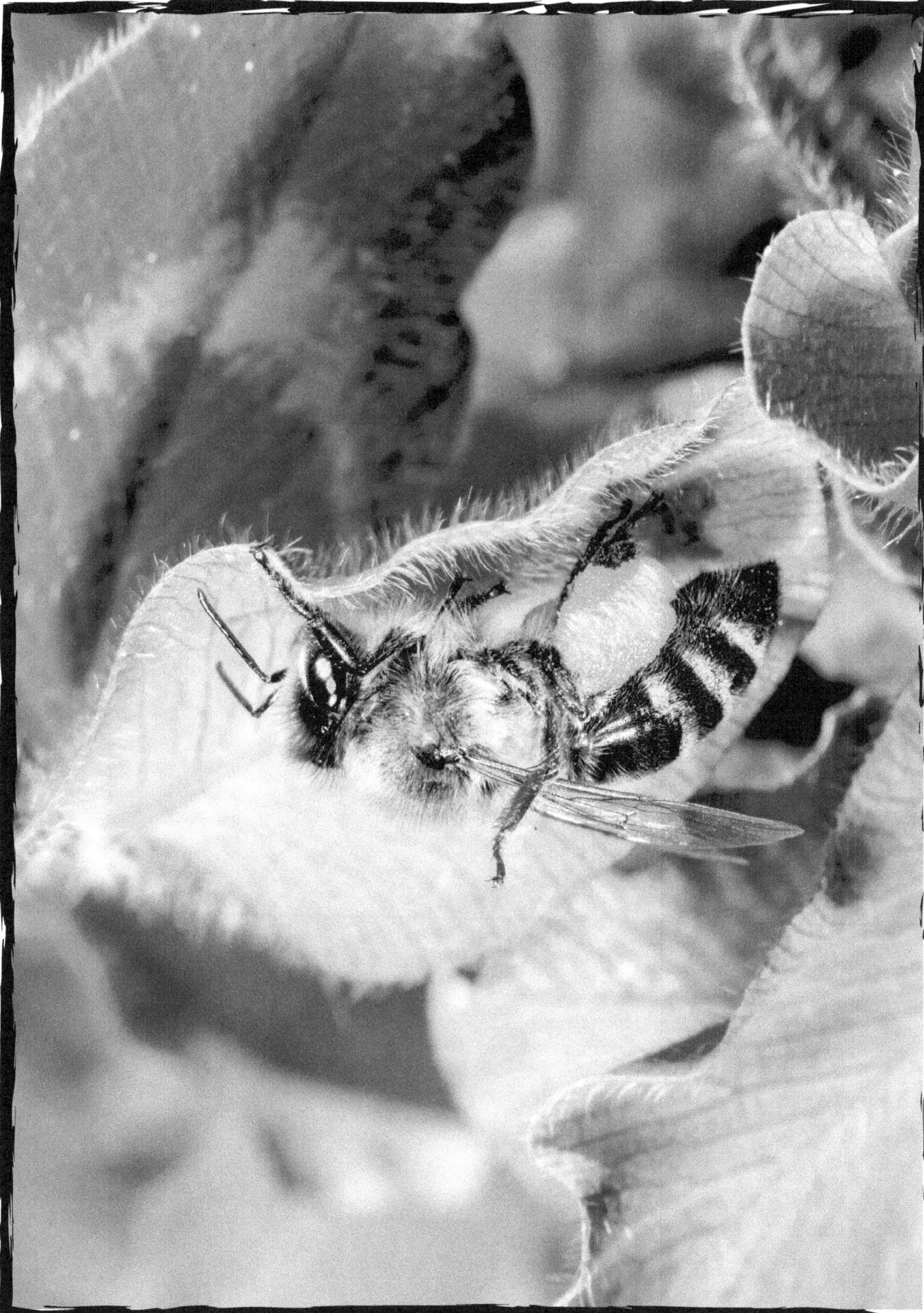

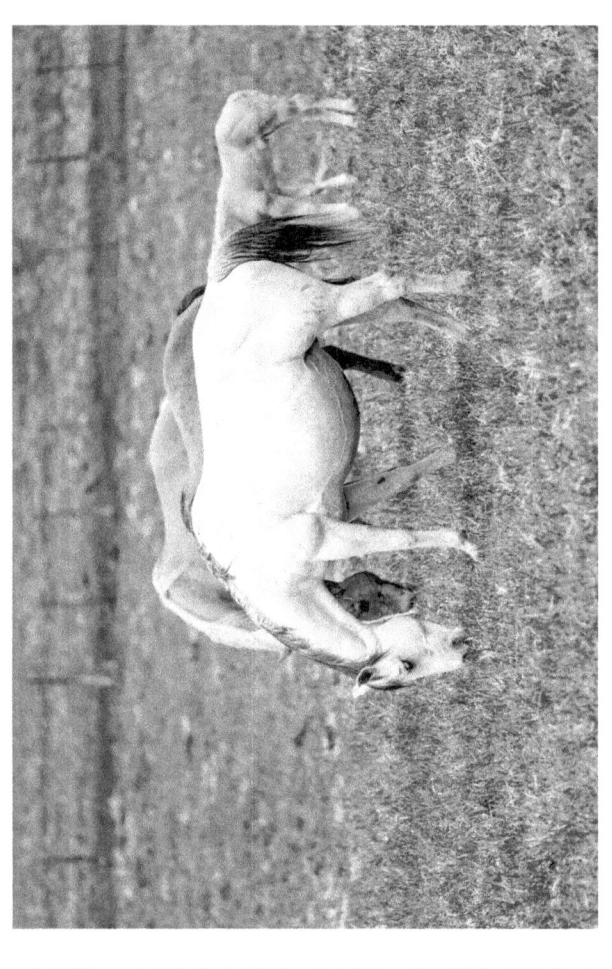
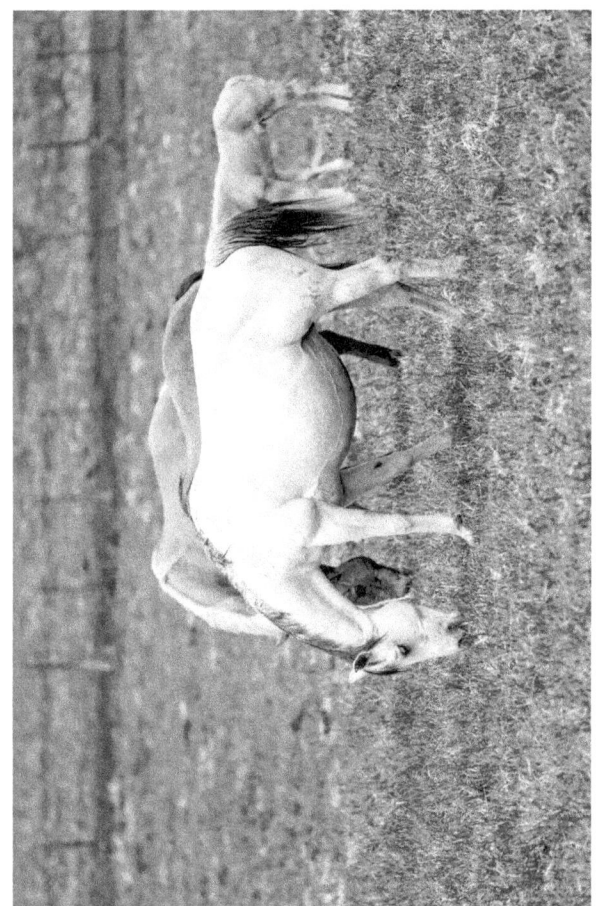
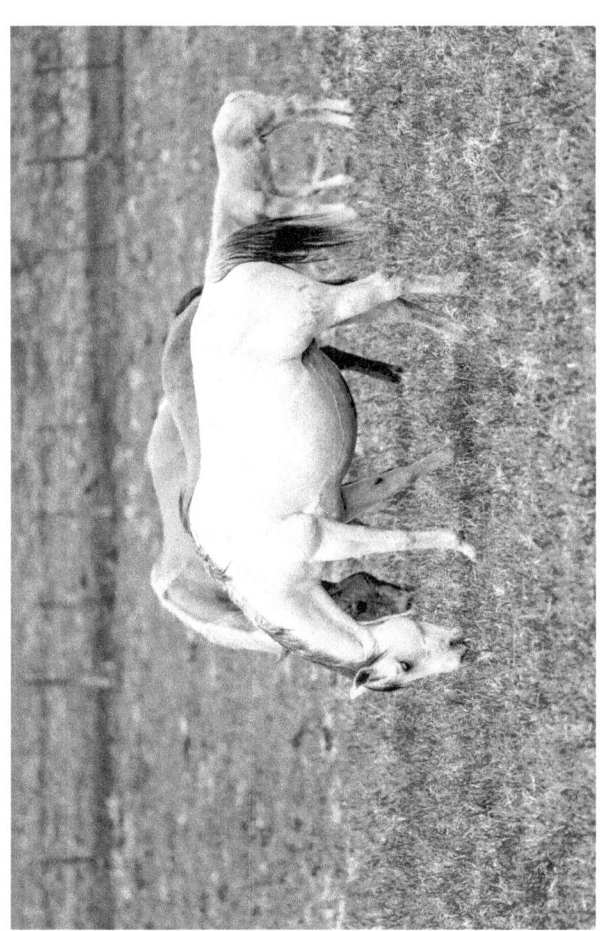
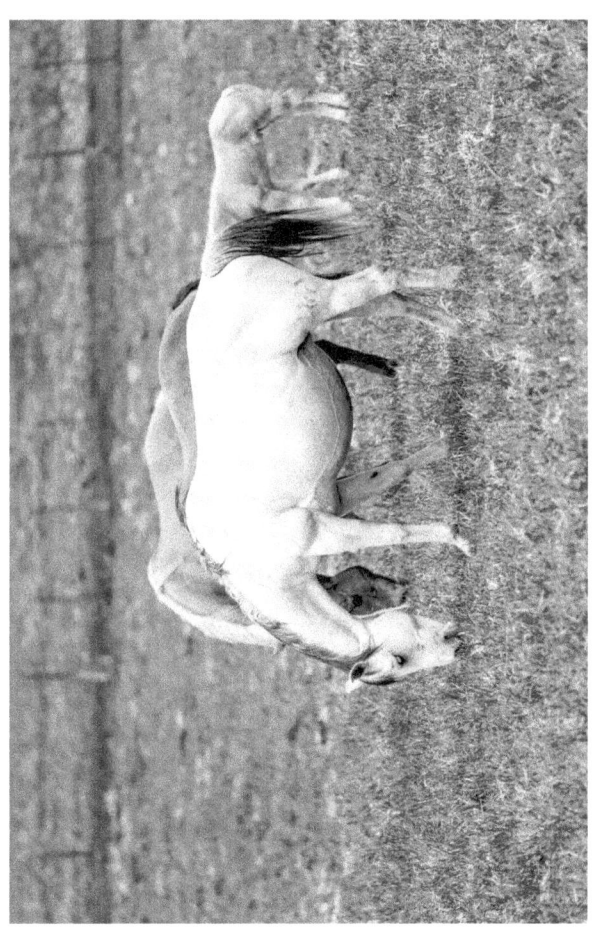

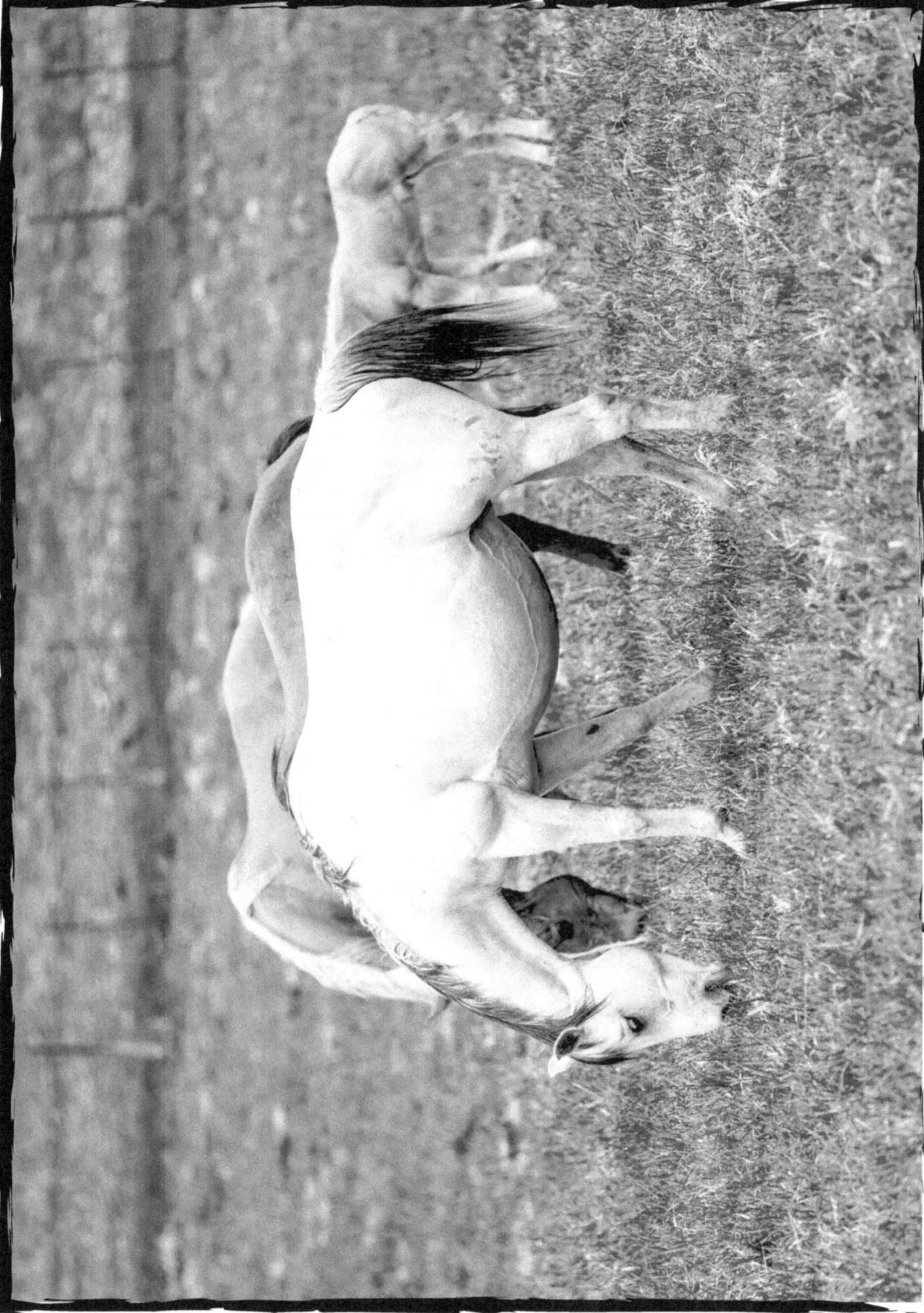

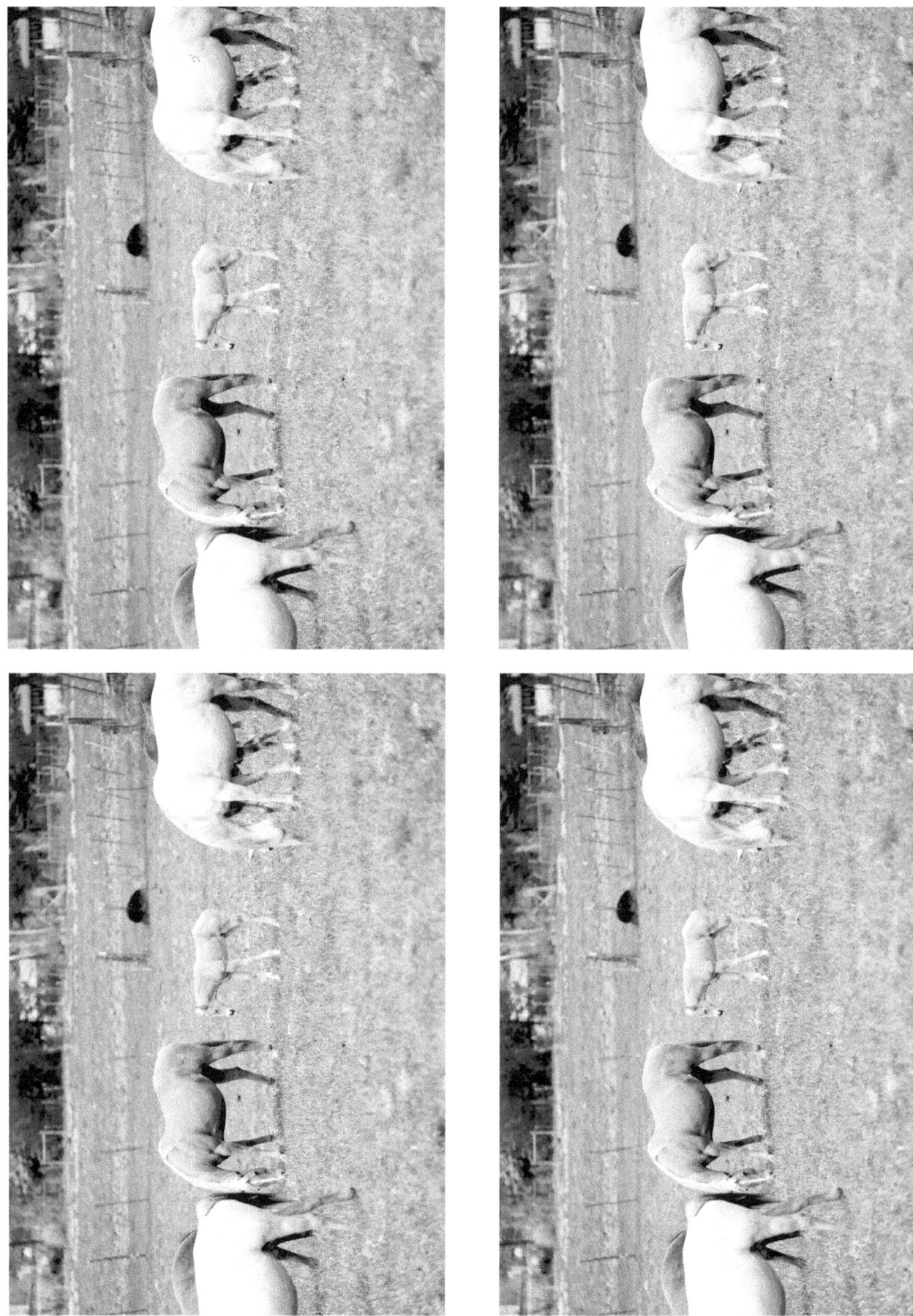

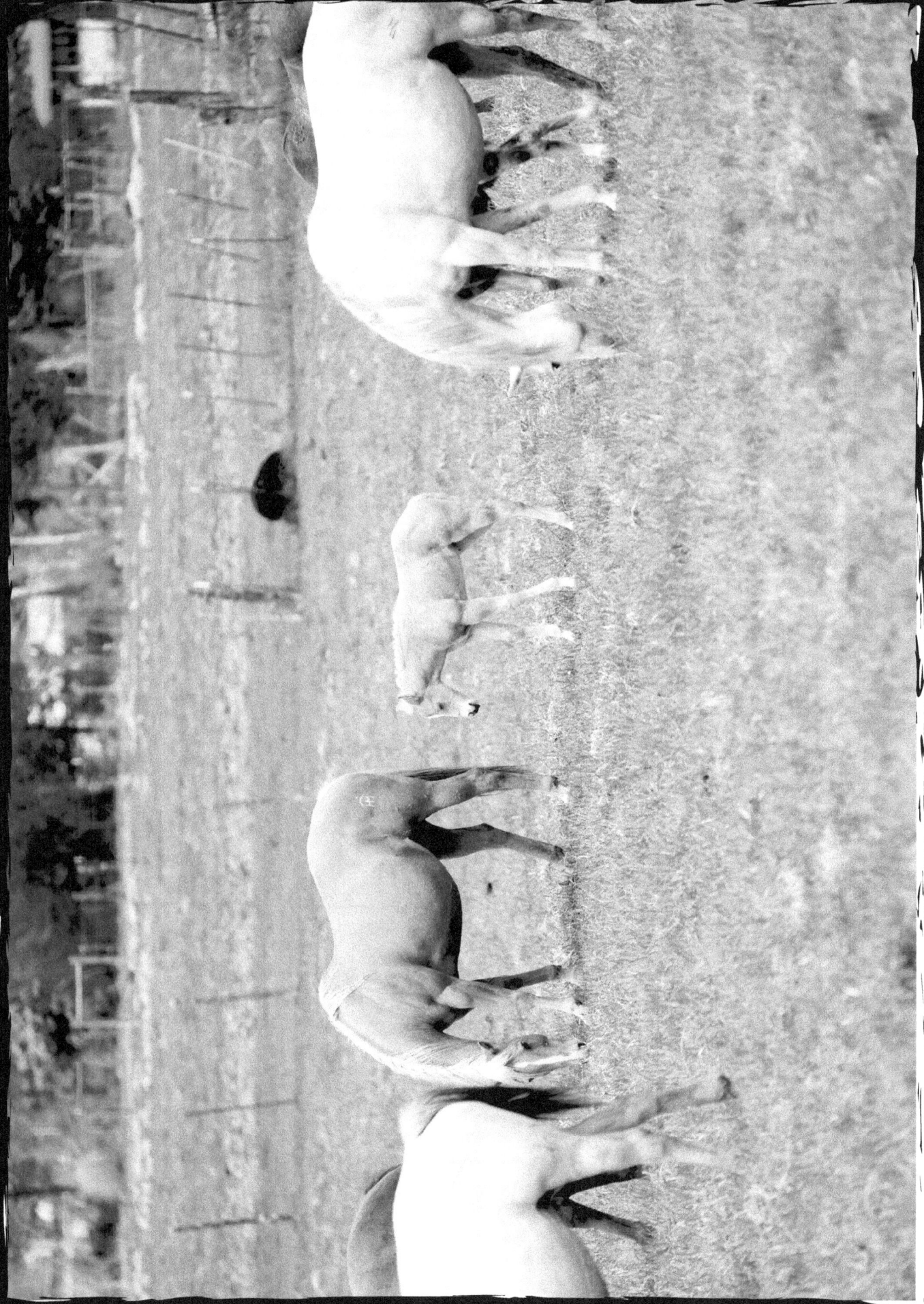

Thanks for picking up a copy of my book. I really appreciate it. If you enjoyed coloring these pages please feel free to leave a review! I would love to hear what you think of my designs.

I would also love to see how you have chosen to color some of my designs. Feel free to email me some pictures of the pages you have colored. You can email me here:

bethingrias@gmail.com

Thanks,
Beth

P.S.
Don't forget to get your free 25 page coloring book at my website.

www.bethingrias.com